Dedicated to the many people who suffer from mental stress, anxiety, PTSD, tremors, and Tinnitus.

I pray you will find your light and come to know the peace that I have found.

We can still be productive and experience happiness in the midst of our own difficult circumstances.

Never give up! Your Light is coming!

II Corinthians 1:3–4
Let this be written for a future generation that a people not yet created may praise the Lord.

—Psalm 102:18, RSVk

Author's Preface

Five days after graduating high school,
I found myself screaming out my General
Orders in a Marine Corps boot camp at
Parris Island, S.C.
In a little over a year, my day often began
with a loud smelly transport by chopper
over the rice paddies of Vietnam, my new
home for the next thirteen months.

Completing my tour of duty
I returned, unwanted, to an ungrateful nation.
And joined the many others experiencing a lifetime of PTSD.

In the midst of constant mental warfare,
I have found writing poetry to be both
challenging and therapeutic.
My relationship with God has never been as fulfilling
as it is now. Through His grace, I look
forward to every moment of life rejoicing in
His wonderful majesty and glory.
I hope that you will be encouraged in mind and
heart; perhaps to write your own poetry
and learn: "It is far better to write than fight!"

A Copper Coin

A very small thing, worth only a fraction;
to some a farthing, to some a mite.
Abolished in time for lack of worth,
thrown upon the ground as value too slight.

Only the poor would claim it as treasure,
found in the purse of a widow or such.
Often overlooked for its usefulness;
like the owner, isn't worth very much.

Yet each coin is watched over money,
in the eyes of the Lord,
for He cherishes it proudly.
To Him, the small is never ignored.

He may catch you giving,
when your own need is great.
He who calls others to notice,
the copper coin in the plate.

                    (Mark 12:41–44)

A Daddy Waits

"Little girl! I'm growing tired of your being late.
My head aches. My palms are sweaty.
I set the time and I'm all ready.
How much more must I accentuate?"

"Little boys are never this much trouble!
I know that there will be many times more,
sitting up late and watching the door;
my nerves are a pile of rubble."

"Why do you challenge me so
at such a young age,
keeping me in this worrisome cage?
That clock on the wall is going way too slow."

"Wait!" The doctor just came in. He made it clear:
"Your wife and baby are fine," he said.
Then I fainted and dropped like a piece of lead.
"Sir, wake up. Your new baby girl is finally here!"

A Father's Love

Created by the Master, His most beautiful of all,
    given the very best and most lovingly caressed.
Ordained companions since the beginning of time,
    the very first to hear His omnipotent call.

Until you discovered desire and other charms,
    and failing the test, you became possessed.
Betrothed rebels chasing the end of your prime,
    you who loosed His hands to grasp other arms.

Confused, in anger, you chose to reject His voice,
    fleeing the nest and finding unending rest.
Never attaining the end of your climb,
    vagabonds imprisoned by deliberate choice.

Your future lies beyond the gates,
    where arriving with zest ever resisting arrest.
Hard labor becomes your newest rhyme,
    the Watcher waits and anticipates.

Note:
* double rhymes in each second line
* third line in each stanza rhyme
* first and last sentence in each stanza rhyme.

A Little White Sheep

Once there was a little white sheep
    who left the fold one day,
not for any bad reason,
    he was just born to stray.

Some thought ill of him,
    certain of his demise.
How would he ever survive,
    with his head so high in the skies?

Always dreaming and looking for adventure,
    he never seemed to fit into any mold.
In time his white wool began turning black,
    and his body growing old.

His steps became slow and weary,
    he often had to stop and pause.
Still, he kept on going,
    determined to find his cause.

Often avoided, misunderstood, and questioned,
    as different as any sheep could be.
Still at the end he bowed his head,
    and prayed this prayer in humility:

"Dear God, I'm still your little white sheep,
    you made me what I am.
And I know you have the power to keep,
    each and every little lamb."

A Love Note

To possess your love in every way,

    to entwine my soul with yours as one,

        to gather memories that fill each day,

            to go through life together as we have done,

                to you I owe much more than I could ever pay.

A New Handle for My Wheelbarrow

If I had a new handle for my wheelbarrow,
I could fix it up,
pump up the tires,
and get a lot more done.

There is that old pile of rocks that I could move.
The ones that are just a little too large
to move by hand,
and it would take all day.

I could place them much more purposefully,
maybe around some of the shrubs
scattered
all over my yard.

There is also that pathway,
the one I started last year,
outlining the sides of the little trail
with rocks I found nearby.

That project kind of evolved
into a pleasant stroll,
leading down to the rose bed
my sweetie worked on so hard.

I bet if I kept on adding rocks,
that wall would look nice
along the back
of the house.

Then, there is that mound of dirt,
I often wished would go away.
Every time I mow the yard,
it just smiles and slows me down.

It's out of place where it is,
and I could use the dirt
to fill up holes
made by uprooted trees.

I could also use the wheelbarrow
to carry some buckets of water
to those plants just out of reach
of the water hose.

I hate to see them reaching out,
thirsty and drying up,
when just an occasional drink
would bring them back to life.

There are so many things
that I could do,
if I just had a new handle
for that wheelbarrow.

It seems like life
is a lot like that handle:
If I had just read a little more,
and had a better vocabulary,

I could have moved
a lot more words
and placed each one
where they needed to be.

Then maybe all my friends
would hang around,
just to sit and talk,
sharing tall tales with me.

A Piece of Sod

Lest any man
    lay claim
        to the glory of God,

Let him first proclaim:
    "I am but
        a piece of sod!"

A Poem to a Weed

Little weed,
you are many times equaled
in breadth and length.
There are many whose climb reaches higher.
But few can know the thoughts you think,
digging into the ground
as you aspire.
What patient hand has made you rare,
and numbered all your days,
nurturing you from seed 'til now,
just so I can see, He rules always?

A Pool That Holds No Water

A pool holds no water,
    whose bottom cannot be found.
Darkness can only deepen,
    when light is still around.

Any destination is reached,
    by that first step taken.
And no distance too great,
    when conveyed by faith unshaken.

Words of wisdom may escape our hearing,
    while the vulgar we proclaim.
But to reach the shores of Heaven's clearing,
    we must enter in Jesus's name.

A Puppy Writes a Poem

I think I would like to see my dog write a poem,
he is much more rested than I.

He surely doesn't know what's cluttering my mind,
the baggage I have to unpack, nor why.

Resting there beneath my feet,
I bet he could probably write a novel.

When for that eternal thought,
I search, and strain, and grovel.

We humans must empty more than bowel,
and fill our cravings with more than food.

We don't scratch just any old itch,
we discriminate, and choose, and brood.

Why can't we be more like my dog,
who sleeps like he has time to kill?

Wagging that tail every time he sees me,
doesn't require one bit of skill.

Yes, I would like to see him write a poem,
but then what does he know?

He would probably grab the pen,
chew up the paper, and off he'd go.

A Shadowed Soul

As a man pursues his dreams
    toward his envisioned mark,
    he too will be pursued.
Each step he takes in faith
    is shadowed by the One,
    he cannot exclude.

The man he was,
    and will become,
    are seldom alike when done.
Whose hand he held,
    most firmly in the dark,
    is there when his race is won.

A Time to Pray

To satisfy the hungry soul,
    one must take time to pray;
        not a prayer in haste,
but the kind of prayer,
    that forgets both night and day.

For whatever cause,
    our knees do bend;
        not a moment should we waste,
because the answer comes,
    in the earnest time we spend.

Until the veil is needed,
    and our radiance shines;
        not until God is faced,
may we depart
    from our closet shrines.

Aging Beautifully

Weeds and leaves and sticks and brush,
    in the lot across the way,
lie strewn in dirt and dust;
    victims of another day.

Yet, I see colors, though faded now,
    yellows, browns, and bits of green.
These soon will disappear,
    no longer to be seen.

Perhaps a bird will come to light,
    on a limb in a tree out there.
To bring some life to that sad place,
    while I'm watching from my chair.

There's that old rusty mailbox,
    propped up on one old spindly post.
I remember when it had purpose,
    now a lonely ghost.

It's strange how we ponder,
    the changes that we see.
Though all the change we would prevent,
    helps to shape eternity.

There is so much beauty,
    in all things new or old.
And when looked upon with purest eyes,
    have value greater than any gold.

An Old Family Album

    Birth

            Rape

                    Miscarriage

                              Abortion

                    Abandonment

            Neglect

    Abuse

            Fear

                 Betrayal

                            Denial

                  Loneliness

            Pain

     Sorrow

            Suffering

                    Discouragement

            Emptiness

     Suicide

            The Funeral

An Old Spider Web

The web was blowing,
a leaf caught in it.
I wondered who the maker,
and how long to spin it.

Would I have chosen
a spot so drear,
then leave my work
to disappear?

Did he not think
to make a plan,
and build his web
the best he can?

That crafty spider,
not like you or I.
But he sure knows
how to catch a fly!

Another Glitch

The fiscal cliff
    has stymied us all,
our politicians leading,
    as the bugler's call.

All the markets
    watched by the world,
with their tattered documents
    begin to unfurl.

The battle is not over,
    we've kicked the can.
A new breath of salvation,
    for middle-class man.

Calendars are marked,
    defining our time,
unique as we are,
    unable to rhyme.

Another Massacre

In the space between life and death,
we find ourselves huddled together,
unsure which direction draws us most.

The places we frequent
have become polluted
with unwelcome noise.

Pops, bangs, and shots ring out;
whose owner possesses
a troubled mind.

We need to throw up,
or cry,
and be held a while.

* Written the day of the Elementary School Massacre in Newtown, Connecticut. Twenty children, ages six and seven, and six adults killed—December 14, 2012.

Another Sermon

Cut away these fruitless branches if you must,
I am old, yet hungry still, in my journey to the dust.
To sit pruned and prideless in this prayed over pew,
is far better than anything else that I could do.

I could be at the beach soaking in the sun,
or enjoying the fresh mountain air having fun.
But I need the food that here I'm fed,
nourished the best on this kind of bread.

There will be beaches in heaven where no sun burns,
and mountains all covered with eternal ferns.
For now I have little time to prepare for such dreams,
for life on earth is not quite as long as it seems.

Just call out the verse, chapter, and book.
I've learned by now pretty well where to look.
Though my Bible is worn and my eyes are weak,
in the Word of God are the riches I seek.

I'll take notes and keep up the best I can,
just help me out where I don't understand.
I don't sing very well anymore but surely will try,
to carry a tune when the angels pass by.

When the offering plate is passed my way,
I'll be prepared because I've saved for this day.
Jesus gets the first, I set it aside,
I love what He does when His love is applied.

The Invitation at the end is the best part for me,
it's my chance to respond and tell Him I see,
the corrections and instructions I need as I wait,
to meet the One worthy past the heavenly gate.

Are There Any More Questions?

I wanted answers to my questions

    for all I desired to know.

But as soon as I reached a conclusion,

    I found I ceased to grow.

Within the questions that we ask,

    the answers are there to find.

Not owned by one, but free to all,

    from one Creator's mind.

Arrow Gant

To my friends it should be expected,
my advice is to be respected.
No other way could we be connected,
until my wisdom you have injected.

To those who deny my contribution,
you deserve swift judgment and retribution.
You could have avoided my premonition,
if you had only heeded my solution.

And now departing I must go,
to dwell above while you're below.
I will seek out others that need to grow,
and bask in the light of all I know.

Becoming Me

Becoming me, I drew from you.
    and though infused we must be two.

I was not shaped in solitude,
    for as life gives we are imbued.

How shall I claim some lofty height,
    except your sway had shaped my plight

I did not choose my mortal time,
    yet here we are that we might rhyme.

Consider this—that though we share,
    unique we are, in need of care.

Of all the deeds that we might do,
    a greater hand has brought us through.

Reward me not for what I've done,
    it was His will who planned our run.

No crown for me to fit my head,
    just you and I sharing bread.

Before Our Time

WHAT IF ALL NATURE JUST STOPPED AND SCREAMED:

"ENOUGH!"

"IT WAS QUITE NICE WHEN ONLY WE WERE HERE.

NOW YOU COME ALONG AND BRING ALL YOUR STUFF,

TO POLLUTE THE ATMOSPHERE.

BE GONE WITH YOU!

WE WILL HAVE OUR REST.

TIMES BEFORE YOU,

AH! THOSE WERE THE BEST."

Beggar on a Corner

Beggar on a corner, holding up a sign:

> WILL WORK FOR FOOD
> VETERAN
> GOD BLESS

Cardboard words speak volumes,
when your life is on the line.

Not much sympathy for these dreamless tramps,
probably raising money for some liquor camp.

Spend more effort avoiding work than looking for a job,
sponging, scavenging, shameless hobo, deceitful fob.

Just getting in the way of an arrogant nose,
like those who drive their shiny cars lined up in rows.

Jeering through the windshields with their pitiful poker faces.
Spurting out a judgment, then off to the races.

Breakfast

I watched her flitter in the kitchen,
    barefoot as she could be.

The cold floor would not stop her,
    from taking care of me.

Bacon frying in the pan,
    "One egg, or two?" she said.

Some grits to fill the tummy too,
    and of course, a slice of bread.

"Coffee's about done, will you fix it, dear?"
    And then she winked at me,
        slumped in my big restful chair.

I did the best I could,
    to help with my little chore.

"Will that be all, my love?" I said,
    "Or will there be something more?"

Then we sat down at the table,
    to eat the meal she had prepared.

And I realized once again,
    just how much she cared.

Being together was the best thing about life,
    never really needing anything more:
"Dear, would you please pass me a knife?"

Bullies

You can make me ashamed, or not very proud,
you can still my voice, or make me loud.
I may think bad thoughts because of you,
but there is one thing you cannot do.

I can be provoked to anger if you dare,
or be frightened by an unexpected scare.
You can make me weep upon command,
but one thing you will never understand.

I know some things you do not know,
whatever happens I will learn and grow.
God made me special, one of a kind,
and you were there when I was on His mind.

Buying New Luggage

The baggage we bring into a relationship,
may spill out along the way.
Embarrassed or praised, we are exposed.

The hurt or hope we carry is also shared;
to our delight or dismay,
we are welcomed or opposed.

So carry your luggage with caution and care,
pack only what you need for today,
and give thanks—Love is never foreclosed.

Cabarrus Creamery

In a historic building in a quaint little city,
known to folks from miles around,
is a place where they make ice cream,
the best homemade ever found.

What used to be a great old mill,
was taken over to build this treat.
Now everyone knows where to go,
to chill on Union Street.

The sights and sounds as you walk in
will surprise the best of connoisseur.
A free-weight gym and an ice cream shop
where fit or fat you may choose your cure.

Most folks want the double,
though single scoops are known.
And the weights in back are handled carefully,
hardly ever dropped or thrown.

Upstairs is a place for art,
a center for the creative mind.
The young and old each share their wares,
a place like this is so hard to find.

Each brick placed so long ago,
sleeps hidden behind the plaster-chipped halls.
Yet still the strength of ages past,
firmly holds valued dreams hanging on the walls.

What a unique mixture is in this place,
colors and materials of all types and sizes.
Everyone that enters leaves with a smile,
thankful that life has so many surprises.

Cain Was My Brother

Throughout my life I carried a cross,
serving as God intended.
The soul inside me was born for such strength,
yet my body grew weaker as each day ended.

Given a will to roam with the flocks,
I received favor when I gave of my best.
Then sorrow and shame came to kneel at my door,
driven from the land and begging for rest.

Opening the door, I let him come in,
downcast and angry, I took up his load.
"Let's go out into the field," he cried:
"Help me regain my stolen abode."

A cloak and staff I took in my hand,
little more did I have worth giving.
With God alone to witness, he took my life,
in the place where we both made our living,

Though the days of my flesh have ended,
my blood cries out from the ground.
Banished and restless, he wanders the earth,
and no man may slay him, lest he too be found.

Circumstance or Contribution?

Like Joseph in Egypt or Esther in Babylon,
your day may not be the one that you prefer;
but with patience and faith you might find,
it may be a contribution that can be depended upon.

The place where you are or your position in life,
may not crown you with peace and happiness;
and there is no guarantee that good things will remain,
for every day contains its share of worry and strife.

Try as you might, pray if you can,
the curse you feel holding on may never change.
What's in you inside must be illumined with light,
as you accept your role in a much greater plan.

Each circumstance can be an opportunity you are given,
to pronounce judgment or proclaim the gift of grace.
Through each deed and every word you have the power,
to create someone's hell or lift them up to heaven.

Climbing Life's Ladder

Life is a journey,
    whether brief or long,
unequal and uneven;
    one continual climb.
We begin on a stairway,
    reaching into heaven.
Our soul drawing us upward,
    our goal sublime.

At first we run,
    and higher we go.
But then we stumble,
    and our steps become slow.
Perhaps a pause here and there,
    even question should we ascend.
Then we rise to continue,
    never looking back to where we've been.

There are many obstacles along the way,
    and a foe of evil to turn us back.
But the angels gather around us,
    and applaud our faithful quest,
If we continue up the ladder,
    We shall meet our blessed Savior,
Whose voice we hear:
    "Enter In, And Rest!"

Conflict over Values

PROPERTY said to PEOPLE one day,
"I've got a great game. Would you like to play?"

So PEOPLE sat down in the chair at his side,
the one with the wheels that easily glide.

He began pressing buttons as he viewed the screen;
being new, he was amazed at how much could be seen.

He applied all his skills, and before he knew,
hours had passed and he still wasn't through.

Exhausted, depleted, he admitted defeat,
his innocence had been taken, there in the seat.

His body ached and he thought it was sad,
no gain was made, no reward, nothing good or bad.

What profit had come from watching the screen
where no human is heard and not one is seen?

Automation and robots will never replace,
Adam and Eve put here by grace.

PEOPLE rose from the chair and left PROPERTY there,
to search for a PERSON and someone to care.

Conflict

Conflict pounces upon the unsuspecting at peace,
bringing words fashioned into weapons;
like greedy vultures feasting on bones.

Circling each weary victim the dark shadows form,
eager to pounce with their talons,
turning each morsel of bread into stones.

From their lofty perch they are hurled,
always in number they gather,
in their pride spewing out lies.

Loyal to no one hearing,
double-minded shadows destroying,
never making any ties.

Fueled by their lust for confusion,
dedicated in fierce devotion,
by their might and size empowered.

Where ignorance and anger have infected,
they stir the opponents into fierce battle,
until even the innocent are devoured.

There is no retreat and no escape,
and when their work is done,
they make certain unfulfilled are all our needs.

No winner is declared,
neither gain nor loss for either side,
while, alone, the beast Conflict feeds.

Country Neighbors

Gray smoke curling upward,
out of the chimney,
blowing a little to the right.
The rust speckled roof,
wet and pale,
drying slowly in the light.

Everywhere brown limbs,
like skeletons,
bending proud and chilled.
Naked stalks and brush
crowded the pond,
anywhere they willed.

There were tall and short hemlocks,
scattered all about
obscuring my view.
The fence posts in formation,
their barbed fingers
painted with a fresh coat of dew.

Cows had been sheltered
into the old barn,
protected from winter's chilly night.
Piles of wood ready for use,
stacked neatly,
uniform and tight.

Fields were light brown,
blanketed with a frosty cover;
here and there a patch of green.
A morning dove cooing softly,
faithful to its maker,
clearly heard yet hardly seen.

Everything a ghostly stillborn,
a vision to be recorded,
everything so carefully placed.
A part of the garden,
sown by God and tilled by man,
ordained when time was chaste.

In the cold I stood there
frozen in frame,
overcome by what I saw.
Why had I not noticed
what now held me
spellbound in awe?

It is always nature's way;
for the young to look forward
while the old look back.
Hidden in the crevice,
pure moments like these,
where no evil may track.

There is not one thing common;
no painted blur of colors,
to come before our eyes.
For each word unspoken,
draws things that fetch us,
when the Master boasts His prize.

It would be a pity
if we dared to spray
in haste this lovely scene.
A loving stroke or two
would be much better
to describe one so serene.

In an instant God had given
a lifetime of happiness,
a memory I will never erase.
I want to carry this picture always
and share it when I can,
another blessing of His grace.

Create

IF YOU ARE THERE

IN THE DARK,

PLEASE COME OUT

INTO THE LIGHT.

EXPOSE YOURSELF

AND ALL YOU ARE,

THAT WE MAY SEE

YOU BURNING BRIGHT.

WE CANNOT RECEIVE

THE GIFTS YOU HAVE

OR SHARE THE JOY

OF ALL YOUR DREAMS,

IF YOU WITHHOLD

SUCH SACRED ART,

AND HIDE YOUR SOUL

IN TIMID STREAMS.

Creations Conflict

Why do folks fuss and argue so,
about creation's timing long ago?
Whoever keeps the record must think it odd,
for man to claim such wisdom would make him God.
Were the stars fixed this way or that?
Was it east or west that first begat?
As we forever struggle, we forever lack,
while the clock of our reason keeps turning back.
In our wonder about what happens tomorrow,
we somehow find a way to borrow sorrow.
Each day anew is filled with fears we face,
so many things we cannot control or erase.
No answer seems to please each fickle round,
where seven days or aeons cannot be found.
Why not trust God, and leave to Him our care?
He who created a time to trust and a time to share.

Creativity

If I were to write what I really wanted,
and not what you expected me to say,
I bet it would make a lot more sense,
and not one syllable would get in the way.

Why sit and think, and think and sit?
Allow the impulses of the heart to beat free.
Then when I am done and cease my words,
you will know less of others, and more of me.

Being original has its benefits,
I believe that was God's design.
Each unique thought makes a contribution,
while influence can stifle the creative mind.

Ever wonder what you could do,
if you let yourself go free?
Think of all the possibilities;
how different the world would be.

Just look at all the works of art,
some master chose to paint.
How beautiful our lives would be,
if we all worked without restraint.

Choose what you love, and do it well,
find your voice, and sing your song.
Pay whatever it cost to buy the tools,
Invest in yourself, you can't go wrong.

Curiosity

With the waking of every dawn,
there are places we are drawn.
Invited there with anxious eyes,
we expect no gain or special prize.
Unclear the reason why we go,
this journey made for us to know.

What makes it burn? We chase the fire.
Above the earth? We must climb higher.
Are there monsters in the sea?
The UFOs, where can they be?
Games we play for their mystique,
and fulfill our lust with sensual peek.

How badly hurt in an accident?
Rubbernecking for some blood or dent.
Hacking or hidden camera; nothing new,
security costs rising; someone's watching you.
It's what we do when bullies bull,
or press to hear a gossip's pull.

Like vultures attracted to death's store,
insatiable appetites wanting more.
In our private seeking we dare to pry,
pursuing rewards never nigh.
How stupefying we all must be;
that uncommon things arouse our curiosity.

Demon's Cannot Fly

Demons are the puppets of perversity,
    with no life in them at all.

They invade the weakened soul,
    and begin to build a wall;

planting lies and distortion,
    they deceive and divide,

causing you to hear things,
    that never have been said.

Conflict and chaos,
    are their most favorite means,

stirring up trouble,
    among the best of friends.

They are slippery little culprits,
    slithering and ever sly,

but we are not afraid,
    because demons cannot fly.

Discontented Man

Wingless bird who longs to soar
above the clouds not seen before.
Fleeing always your regretful past,
yearning for new life to make it last.
Struggling to possess the utmost power,
cannot rule thyself one precious hour.

Cry a little the tearless flow,
so many places you did not go.
Having looked into so many eyes,
reflecting pools to the unwise.
Floundering through life with choices made,
ever struggling beneath thy father's shade.

Can thy quest find rest in another sphere,
what starward gaze would yet appear?
What deity beside you standing,
finds honor in the deeds of his demanding?
Your days are fashioned in discontent,
where unfulfilled dreams are never spent.

Done

Daily, I am diminished,
    and it saddens me so.
The boardwalk of life has shortened,
    my steps are growing slow.

Many friends have left me,
    alone on the shore.
gazing at another horizon,
    beckoning like an open door.

The winds of time,
    compete with the sanded clock,
ever pushing me into strange waters,
    farther from this finite dock.

Frail is the balance,
    that welcomes the end.
Yet my soul ventures homeward,
    I hear the calling of a friend.

Dwelling in Our Differences

You thought I was being bad,
when all the time
it really wasn't so.

I believed in good,
I sought pure goals
until I had to go.

There is a devil out there,
who is always sowing seeds
trying to cast us down.

He comes to dwell in our differences,
when we each defend our space,
and arrogantly stand our ground.

Our pride makes us build a wall;
the price is way too high,
and both of us will pay.

When we join the multitudes
like betrayed fiends
and choose to stay away.

We bear his scars.
you and I,
and live our lives apart,

But it is my dream,
that someday soon we'll be,
rejoined together, heart to heart.

Equality

Those who struggle for equality
    run the risk of their own demise.
Obtaining equality dissolves identity,
    and leaves a speck in each man's eyes.

God has made things all diverse,
    to Him each seed is pure.
To try to change the universe,
    confuses things for sure.

We may supply each other's need,
    and honor each different gift,
if we empty ourselves of vain pride and greed,
    giving uniqueness and unity a little lift.

Eternity
(Job 19:23–27)

Let my words reach you,
teach you from the grave.
May this I have recorded
be the best I ever gave.
This that you are now reading;
these words I once had spoken,
verifies our shared hope,
and life goes on unbroken.
I am in you,
and you are in me.
The spirit is alive
in all of Eternity.
Let all life exalt the Lord,
and may praise rise from everyone.
In Him all things exist,
from Him all things begun.
Bound are we together,
forever closed the gap.
Redemption is our Savior,
abiding in the Master's lap.

Evidence for Life

It is time for a tear,

    though I have none.

Just one tiny trickle of clear,

    down my cheek to run.

I wish my heart would please my eye,

    and release the tender spill.

Am I so hardened that I can't cry,

    like a stone; cold and still?

Useless and lifeless,

    unable to respond?

All must not be ended,

    nor empty the pond!

Faith and a Gangplank

Exercising faith is like walking a gangplank.
We step out to take that frightening walk
and find ourselves alone and afraid.
As duty demands, we venture to the edge.

Recounting the purpose for which we've come,
a dialogue erupts in soul, and mind, and heart,
where far too much time is spent measuring doubt.
Given a gentle nudge, we spy a glance across the ledge.

The time comes when we know we must take that leap,
for the pain of any turn echoes a failed and faulty plan.
A death must occur when our faith is most tried,
with one step for truth, we enter into the unknown.

The fall we feared does not occur as we expected,
since by the gravity of sin we are drawn no more.
We rise through the clouds held in the arms of angels,
singing their comforting song: "You were never alone!"

Fallen Angels

Like trees with severed trunks are we,
broken limbs, our baggage of regrets.
To weak to persevere and overcome,
blaming others for our lack and debts.

We gather around our pagan friends,
who keep the sun from shining through;
failing daily to struggle upward,
as we were designed to do.

Precious leaves escape our shaky arms,
as time goes fleeting by.
We produce no fruit for anyone,
if all our effort goes to asking: WHY?

Fate and Faith

Light breaks forth from darkness,

    never darkness from the light.

Hope springs forth Eternal,

    as Faith puts Fate to flight.

Field and Streams

If no man shares my dreams,
I make my friends of field and streams.
When all are gone and I'm left alone,
I'll rest my head on beds of stone.

I take my bath in the rain and dew,
and dry my bones in a sunrise new.
What dirt I shun is the evil deed,
truth will be the only book I read.

Let no one mock or shame my plan,
though he may envy my caravan.
Flocks and herds, wild beasts, and fish,
all do eat from nature's dish.

The roads I travel are roads not worn,
but happy trails of the innocent born.
No trash or litter to defile the way,
just blooming bouquets in scattered array.

Come, go with me and let us explore,
you need not wear conformity anymore.
Strut your stuff and be yourself,
only things out of circulation are put on a shelf.

Flesh and Spirit

Two worlds living inside me, unalike and unknown;
flesh and spirit, seeded before my birth.
Like two hands reaching out to nourish,
vying for my final worth.

Oftentimes in opposition,
dividing up my soul.
While the peace in their union,
ignites the spark that makes me whole.

Perhaps they are not two warriors warring,
but two cherubs at my side.
Watching over the ark of God,
wherein dwells His holy bride.

For My Son

Mosquitos, flies, and bumblebees,
allergy shots and bandaged knees.
    complaints and giggles,
    little bug that wiggles.
Catch the ball,
try not to fall.
    A pool to splash,
    a summer's bath.
Untied shoes and dirty socks,
Cycling wobbly on driveway rocks.
    Quit that tugging at your ear,
    new habits born in every year.
Thank God for you and heaven,
and pray for me, 'cause you're only seven.

Forgiven

I heard the roaring thunder,

    I saw the lightning flash.

Standing there in wonder,

    I surveyed my past.

The words I feared so long,

    I knew were soon to come.

The time had come for reaping,

    for the things that I had done.

The darker path I had chosen,

    my steps were swift to go.

Each day as I got older,

    I still refused to grow.

I did not heed the warning,

    only my rules would I obey.

I was so often selfish,

    greed and pride led me astray,

No more time for running,

    or hiding in the dark.

The Truth had come like morning,

    the arrow hit its mark.

In the twinkling of an eye,

    I was standing before the throne.

Where the Judge of one and all,

    meets every man alone.

I knew I was a sinner,

    I bowed my head in shame.

Was there no one to save me?

    I searched for hope to claim.

        (pause)

From my dream, I came awake,

    a reprieve was given me.

The dream I dreamed had been a warning,

    eyes once blind now could see.

I had not known the Lord,

    I could only see my sin.

Right there in my confession,

    a light came breaking in.

I bowed to the One before me,

    I cried out His holy name.

There in my surrender,

    His child I became.

Found Beneath Our Feet

Peeking out from behind their darkened doors,
are many different gems, planted when earth began.
Buried among stones, deep in the soil,
waiting on shovel, and pick, and pan.

The master craftsman comes with watchful eye,
cutting away unneeded material and letting in light.
Until each obtains its most valuable glow,
one of a kind with every facet just right.

The strength of these gems are tested by fire,
their luster and brilliance rely on reflection.
Adorning the home of a worthy soul,
is grace sufficient to make the right connection.

Though there are dark recesses that we may fear,
we are the diadems that God wants to keep.
Our faith will lead us through each wilderness,
for He has both crown and cup to reward His sheep.

Free Will

While passing through this life,
we sometimes taste forbidden fruit,
never stopping to ask for permission.

Yet we continue to live each day,
discovering a healing kind of grace,
that saves us from each wrong decision.

God grants to every one of us,
His free will each day we are living,
until we approach His open arms,
to find the worth of true forgiving.

He heals our pain, our grief, and loss,
and casts away all doubt and shame,
where arriving at His throne we dwell,
eternally united in His name.

The cost of grace for our rebellion,
only God could bear alone,
to give His Son for each man's sin,
and right the wrongs that we have done.

What patient Love that God bestows;
His faithfulness beyond our sight,
let us choose to turn from wrong,
and walk the path of unearned Light.

Freedom

Man may not worship who he thinks he can,
that question was resolved before earth began.

Who we worship is not a freedom God has given,
to divide up the gods is idol worship and devilish sin.

With freedom to worship, man attempts to make it all fair,
and with freedom from worship, he proposes to care.

How little we grow, how feeble we walk,
not knowing who is to listen and who is to talk.

No man is free before he knows God,
even death is a chain that binds him to sod.

God gives freedom to the born-again soul,
and then gives them heaven, eternities goal.

"Worship the Lord your God, and serve him only" (Matt. 4:10).

Friends

Man has few friends in this life,
they need not be cut from the same cloth as he.
Their gifts, like currents, can challenge his course,
or brightly light his path upon whatever sea.

While tested by the praise we receive,
the wounds of a friend we may trust.
Humble and honest he bears his heart.
where we know his counsel is just.

A sharper iron may no one find,
than one forged by a friend.
Chosen by God, more than animal or plant,
was Man from Beginning to End.

(From Proverbs 27)

From the Manger to the Marriage

Is there a place where we can go
bearing gifts of value beyond compare
that never before have been seen?

Perhaps to a manger in some lowly place,
prepared through time and careful thought,
in a house of bread, secluded and serene?

We've traveled through harsh lands of slavery,
a wilderness of many wars and tribulations,
each turn leaving us lonely and afraid.

Ever beckoned by a star of hope,
we walked the sacred tablets of time,
through faith was each step made.

The cattle on a thousand hills,
belong to Him;
the One we long to meet.

As purely fashioned as we can,
we will bow and place our offering,
in humility and obedience at His feet.

A wedding marks our journey's end,
beyond death lies the door.
His resurrecting power prevails always,

We have an invitation
to gather around His throne
and sing the bridal song of praise.

Funeral for Love

What happens to Love,
    if we no longer let it grow?

Have you stopped to think,
    or do you know?

Love can't be shelved,
    or put away.

To return, perhaps
    another day.

It cannot be replaced,
    or even die.

To believe Love goes,
    would be to lie.

Gettysburg

Over the ridge they came,
I heard their swearing.
As we fired—they fell,
into the past of a mean uncaring.

Might some have been brothers;
young boys, or old men?
Death's rattle makes all equal,
as it welcomed them in.

Soon the smell overcame the swearing,
mangled bodies littered the field.
The smoke cleared—the earth more clouded,
revealed its hellish yield.

Which side had won this day in battle?
Would forever the wrong be made aright?
Is there in the making of a hero,
this needed darkness come to light?

Mourned with some honored words,
so many lives less important than the cause.
Unknown soldiers will not be remembered,
It is the site made sacred by applause.

No one will call them "father",
even their laughter is silenced now.
Diminished and empty we march forward,
to some other cause we must endow.

Going Spiritual

If you ever want to go spiritual, may I suggest:
    Go SILENT!
        Go STILL!
              Go VERY SLOW—DO NOT STOP!
           DO NOT GO TO SLEEP!
         ONLY LISTEN,
                UNTIL YOU'RE EMPTY!

Gossip

It takes a combination of thoughts

    to form an attitude,

where judgments are made incorrectly,

    and indelibly crude.

Those who judge are fully infected,

    and like the tiny mite,

spread their diseased information,

    with every single bite.

Half-Truths

Half-truths are verses of perversity;
corruptions of the original Script,
creating havoc and chaos;
spawn from a foul ethereal crypt.

Ever since the beginning of time,
when the Word was spoken as Truth,
half-truths were cunningly seeded,
to rob mankind of his youth.

More is spoken that is half-true,
than all the books could hold;
division, doubt, and destruction,
the spun web of counterfeit gold.

In each judgment made by man,
through a virus comes the hacking,
to infect all of God's creation,
and corrupt the hope that's lacking.

Light has come from darkness,
the Truth given birth to reveal,
half-truths lustful pleasure,
and prove its plan unreal.

If any dare to speak as God,
he must know the enemies power.
The life He gave, He took up again,
to judge half-truths final hour.

To set out to right the wrongs
that always find a cup to fill,
one must know his heart is true,
and his guide is Love's perfect will.

Harken to the Trumpet

How deeply hurt
    must a soul know pain,

before life expires
    and there's no more gain?

Must the song of sorrow
    play loudest of all,

in the echoed silence
    of the mourner's call?

Where is hope when all seems gone
    and torment envelopes like a shroud?

Just keep reaching out to the Unknown God,
    He is coming through the cloud!

Healing the Sick

Except we learn through sorrow,
    until we prevail o'er pain,
we dare not face tomorrow,
    and make no greater gain.

For those chosen to know the Way,
    fully yielded to God's plan,
steps are directed to His throne,
    leaving behind the mortal realm of man.

Humility prays the greatest prayer,
    for it understands the cost of pride.
The soul offered up to Him in care,
    will be seated by His side.

Curing comes through caring,
    more deeply than most know.
But rest assured it happens,
    the healer knows the way to go.

His and Hers

We've come a long way, out threads are thin and bare,
from too much hanging around, with little time to spare.
It's good to have a pal, a friend, a little help now and then;
more now than ever, considering the shape we've gotten in.

We've been through the wringer several times before,
and chances are, we will be in a little more.
No one could match up to us, the work we do;
we're a set for sure, even though we're far from new.

With a swipe here and a wipe there, we clean a lot of mess.
"Cleanliness is next to godliness" is the motto we confess.
When comes that day, and we are folded and put away,
will we be honored with thanks or flowery bouquet?

What greater reward could there ever be,
than to warm each other in close proximity.
When we are finally laid to rest,
Each of us will say: "We did our best!"

His Voice Is Calling

The One guiding me is unknown and unseen,
    yet forevermore abiding in my soul.
As I age, my body grows weak beyond my will,
    the still small voice keeps me remaining young.

When these two friends depart; my body and this life,
    gently guide me and beckon me on.
May this be an unbroken end,
    lest I upon some cross am remaining hung?

Passion and desire in me were harnessed late,
    and the race was swiftly run.
The choices I made have altered me,
    my confession I bring openly wielding.

Like a ship tossing about on troubled waters,
    off course at times, yet never defeated.
I was always guided to some better shore,
    assured by One not yielding.

The Lord is my hope, in Him will I trust,
    and when the last step of faith I have taken;
when I lie down and draw my last breath,
    may it be His face I see when I awaken.

Homeless People

"Why are homeless people homeless?"
someone once asked of me.
"Well, sit down," I said,
"and I think you will see."

A lot have become addicted,
to drugs or drink.
It cost them family and friends,
and infected the way they think.
They lost where they lived,
and were asked to leave.
Now they are without a home,
leaving behind loved ones to grieve.

Then, there are the mental,
whose minds are just not right.
Often poured out of an overrun mental institution,
they seek shelter for the night.
These are very noticeable
by those who pass them by.
"There but for the grace of God"
we hear folks say, "Go I."

There are those who are just lazy and irresponsible,
who only know how to take and never give.
They had a home until they drained every resource,
of those who kept the place where they used to live.
With no one to feed them, or clothe them,
or carry them off to bed,
they wind up on the streets,
with not much promise ahead.

Last of all are those who are truly homeless,
suddenly without work or down on their luck.
Some overwhelming crisis caught them all alone,
wiping away everything, some hurricane struck.
Bewildered, they too, wander the streets,
until some good Samaritan happens by,
willing to offer genuine help to restore and rebuild,
someone loving enough to say: "Together, we will do it, you and I."

Homeless

Looking deeply into his eyes,
I saw the soul of a broken man.
His only friends: loneliness and despair.
Loitering through life with no thought to plan,
trespassing in a world much too busy to care.
No zeal, no lust, for any cause,
identity and credentials long gone.
Expressions of faith, none to display,
so many things he had left undone.
An empty case where once an instrument lay;
needing, yet never needed.
Naked, with nothing to own,
ever pursuing the grave.
A sad epitaph to carve on a stone:
"His end was the best that he gave."

(I worked in a Homeless Shelter in Pennsylvania for several years.)

Hoping for Heaven

Dear Lord up in Heaven,

It sounds too good to be true.

Is there really a Heaven,

and an Eternity with you?

My soul is longing to see,

Oh! To be your guest.

Please allow me to enter

Thy peace and thy rest.

How to Know Your Faith Is the Best?

You will know your faith is the very best,

    when it can pass the purest test.

The test of truth that is superior to all others,

    where One will stand supreme among His brothers.

You can know your faith is better,

    than all the rest,

because only Christ wants what is best,

    for all the rest!

Humility

When humility envelops us
    like a shroud,
accept us, O Lord,
    up through some cloud.
When given white robes,
    by Your gracious choice,
may we wave our palms,
    as You hear one voice:

"Salvation belongs to our God,
who sits on the throne,
and to the Lamb."
    (Revelation 7:9–10)

I Am Looking for a Family

For the rest of my life my energy will be spent
on finding me a family that I can love.

It seems that those of my own dear blood
are far more distant than many strangers that I meet.

To share a smile or simply take the time to really listen
seems to be something my kin know little of.

So many choices are given in this life,
perhaps in choosing our family we make our lives complete.

I need a family who will not neglect, abuse, or abandon.
Is there anyone out there you know?

I've met some really great people along the way.
We seem to share most openly the depths of heart and soul.

Without labor, we accept one another as we are
and do not have to walk on egg shells as we go.

Yes! I think I will seek a family among good folk.
In fact! It shall become my brand-new goal.

I Can Always Tell

I cannot always tell you
when a word should be spoken,
but I can tell you
when a word I should not say.

I cannot always tell you
what I am supposed to be doing,
but I can tell you
what I am not allowed to do.

I cannot always tell you
where I am supposed to be,
but I can tell you
where I am not supposed to go.

If in the course my race I've run,
and my gains are more than less,
this tribute to my past I give:
I've learned right much about success.

I Long to Write

It is time for my soul

    to seek its pleasure again,

and plunge me into that place

    where no one else can enter in.

There where I am the most complete,

    finding solace in that sweet retreat.

To write whatever I may choose,

    while courting only the sacred muse.

Unleashing thoughts without a care,

    for hope lives beyond this earth's despair.

Untouched by fear of invasive eyes,

    driven in earnest toward completion's prize.

If Not for Mercy

The BODY, like an empty container,
is planted in dust or cast into the fire.
Our hope depends upon a gracious God,
for each man's time will soon expire.

The challenged MIND calls forth thought,
connecting choice to consequence, like dot to dot.
Such reaping and sowing, forgetting and knowing,
guides daily our active lot.

The fickle HEART juggles devotion and desperation,
pulsing with life each beat ordained.
For the fool and wicked, the wise and pure,
The heart is where the treasure is maintained.

The SOUL is the keeper of the palace,
the temple where man meets with God.
Granting forgiveness in unique fashion,
judging between the real and the fraud.

The parts don't stay together,
unless they are renewed.
Even then that depends,
upon God's certitude.

If You Fix My Soul

Through the thickest of thorns
I struggle along,
scratched, yet murmuring,
I sing my song.

"O let me be merry and gay,
as I proceed along my way."

If I could just be a little kind,
a wound to heal, a hope to bind,
a word well said, a way made known,
some good to share, a vine well grown.

"O let me be merry and gay,
as I proceed along my way."

To kneel and help a small frail child,
love every creature tame or wild.
Let love burst from the scars I bear,
each breath I take pure cleansing air.

"O let me be merry and gay,
as I proceed along my way."

Dispel the darkness and bring the light,
I'll take each wrong and set it right.
I must be guided by some greater hand,
beyond my power to understand.

"O let me be merry and gay,
as I proceed along my way."

If you fix my soul and comfort me,
renew my strength and set me free,
my praise I'll give and my consent,
each blessing as my life is spent.

"O let me be merry and gay,
as I proceed along my way."

(Written to overcome depression—a Vietnam Vet.)

Ignorance and Faith

In ignorance I stray,
in faith I follow,
two paths unknown;
friend or foe.

One leads to sin,
with the other I serve;
both bothered by doubt,
each my soul unnerve.

Born in grace,
raised in mercy,
growing in obedience,
as the seeds are sown.

May it be for God's glory,
this life may I live,
my soul going upward,
I've finally learned how to give.

Images in My Head

There are images in my head;
images not of peace but of war.
Places I choose not to visit,
I don't want to go there anymore.

Looking at the wall,
this monument of stone.
I weep for those whose journey ended,
so far away from home.

While looking at each name,
the thought that passes slowly by:
Why was life not traded,
that they should rest, not I?

Imagination

Such a powerful thing;
unseen.
Pillar of the mind;
with thoughts,
clean and not clean.
Leaflets blowing in the wind;
inviting dreams,
igniting schemes.
Seen by angels;
abiding,
guiding.
Dry bones without frame;
building a fire,
desire.
Open doors of prisons;
premeditation,
incarceration.
Naked tomorrows;
starving,
bewildering.
Taking flight swiftly;
leaving,
grieving,
feral,
sterile.

Jesus Came to Church

I saw Him come in,
    when you opened the door.
He placed His hand upon your back,
    as you walked down the aisle.

The church where all can come,
    to be healed and restore.
And when you took a seat,
    you should have seen His smile.

I could see from where I stood,
    and wondered if you knew,
how pleased He was,
    to sit beside you in the pew.

He watched you sing and pray,
    and saw your tears of sympathy
for the hurting and the needy,
    and the lost who did not see,

He will rise with you and heal them all,
    when you are ready to begin.
Yes, Jesus came to church today,
    because you let Him in.

John the Baptist

Take a seat and sell your wares,
    the wind swayed reed is bound.
His palace is sand, his sandals worn,
    his clothes are poor and earthen wound.

The Way he knows and opens doors,
    no one born will more honored be.
Though he declare your coming time,
    you lifted his head in revelry.

Supposing demons had o'ertaken him,
    his followers you feared the most.
Holding rather to the laws you made,
    shunning even the latter Host

Play your flute and dance your dance,
    untouched is earth by your lament.
Wisdom's child will be your judge,
    To hell your way is bent.

He who rightly prepares the way,
    has a home in heaven for him,
To eternally wear a golden crown,
    and sit among the cherubim.

Just Being Me

Though no man knows my script,
    nor any man my walk;
not one word has been summoned,
    and in freedom do I talk.

With allegiance to none but God;
    being cast out upon life's sea,
uniquely framed and fueled by grace,
    I did my best at being me.

To those I may have offended,
    with a word I chose to speak,
I must have thought it truth to say:
    if offended, they were weak.

I responded to each challenge,
    unlike any other might.
Accepted shame for being wrong,
    yielding to those who choose to fight.

I sought no great glory,
    from responsibility tried never to flee.
With courage as my breastplate,
    I did my best at being me.

Just Old Books

My hungry eye, all by itself,
found these things high upon a shelf.
Surprised to find them where they were,
calling out to the inquiring adventurer.
In an antique shop itself quite old,
where treasure hunters go to dig for gold.
The dust had gathered because of neglect;
the dust of ignorance, I really suspect.
Not glass, nor plate, or silverware,
old metal toy trucks, or luminaire.
These were the thinkers and poets of the past,
bound in the coffins that history had cast.
Volumes amid columns competing for profit,
numbered spaces filled with wood or writ.
Books meant to be read were placed out of sight,
sadly, things hard to ponder often let in most light.
That all the great poets, who set things to rhyme,
could become discarded debris in the annals of time.
I thought of the future, I thought of myself:
How long until classified and put on a shelf?
Sold for nickels and dimes, their value diminished,
hallowed word passed down, and work unfinished.

Just Us Three

"Right now, there's just us three,
I reckon that's all we need to be.
When called upon, our purpose is slight,
binding together and making things tight.
We never try to question our part,
So proudly become our master's art.
Useful tools, we help to create,
doing our work and never late.
Never a complaint, no leaves for the sick,
just binding locks, a thoughtful trick.
Vacations and days off seldom come about,
for we refuse contention to sprout.
We love our part and ask for no more,
just three hair rollers, keeping hair off the floor."

Laborers and Lords

I gots me a bucket
    I'ze got plenty a watah
        an I gots me a hose.
Don't need much nuttin' else,
    maybe a little soap,
        an a lot a hard work.
Work dat makes da sweat fall
    down in yo eyes.
Fact is, I sometimes works so hard
    dat I nearly falls down.
But, I ain't stoppin'. No sir!
    Not til' dat shine comes thru.
        It all gots ta be real purty,
Jes' da way I knows it can be,
    Dat car goin be da envy a everybody.
        People come from miles around,
        to see dat shine.
I bet dat car go even faster,
    when I gits thru.
        jes' cause that shine is so slick.
I make sho' it don't have one spot
    dat ain't clean.
Even dem tires looks new,
    you watchem shine.
You can see yo'sef in it,
    like a mirror,
If'n you stands real close.
    you can see yo' smile.
Don't matter if da car ain't mine,
    I could never 'ford anything so fine.
        No sir! Don't matter a 'tall.

Ownin' it ain't mine to do,
    my part is to jes' keep it clean,
   I jes' makes it shine!

* Written in honor of a dear old friend I knew when I was a young paperboy many years ago. My first awareness of age and persons of other color. I've never forgotten the beauty in his life.

Leah

Sprawling kiss curls and a pink tutu,
accompanied by her circus cat.
Long blond hair,
blue eyes and a birthday hat.

We watched in awe,
as she danced across the floor.
Was she five or six?
I don't remember anymore.

That great big smile,
and charm to hypnotize.
So much energy,
for someone her size.

Independent and a little stubborn,
a recipe of mommy and dad.
So determined and bright,
and hardly ever bad.

Ahead of her time in earning wings,
a tender heart at home with peace.
Touched by God this special gift,
ours to watch while the days increase.

I just wish
we could stop her growing.
But there are so many others,
she needs to be knowing.

So we thank God,
for the time we're given to share.
Photographed in our memories,
she will always be there.

Legacy of a Teacher

My life was given

I've come to know,

to make you think,

perhaps to grow.

Let Us Not Be Weary in Well Doing

I looked for a cause,
    something good to be done,
and found the course toughened,
    the battle not easily won.

Many stars have been followed
    by those hopeful and wise,
only to be stilled,
    over deceit in disguise.

There is a star leading,
    to the pure and the whole.
Wait for its brightening,
    to illumine your soul.

Heavenly host will worship,
    and Truth will attest,
the choice made in sacrifice,
    and doing right is always best.

Persevere though you've been beaten,
    pause but do not stop.
call for help if it's needed,
    for the cross you must not drop.

Life Is a Journey

Suppose you were to go on a journey to a place far away,
traveling by foot, or whatever means came your way.
What if you took all the Yearning and Passion you could carry
in your pack, never knowing when you would return,
or what you would bring when you came back?

How far would you go; what investment would you make,
to insure you reached your destination for the pilgrimage
you had to take?

Perhaps to the sea where pearls and shells and the ageless
sands of time delight. Or to some lofty mountain peak,
given nature's goal to gain the greatest height.

Maybe across unexplored virgin territory, going at
Olympic pace. Or hurtling like a meteor, throughout the
vast reaches of space.

What price would you be willing to pay for the experience
you would gain? Would you cash your ticket in if the
journey required too much pain?

Such a journey is asked of each one of us, and many times
a day. Though most choose to quickly turn, avoiding to go
the narrow way.

Drugged by our own private addictions, we often escape and
miss the call, never recognizing the disease creeping in that
keeps us weak and small.

Life offers its best challenge, when we are asked to grow.
How far, how high, what price would you pay to go?

Little Chicaboom

Stubborn little dainty so fully alive,
busy little bee, encircling the hive.
Where does your spirit soar to now?
unpredictable and mysterious faie art thou.
A sparklet from the wishing wand,
unending zeal ever going beyond.
Measured from the cup of a father's love,
beauty in likeness to the mother dove.
How we resemble, you and I,
when seeing the two, none can deny.
You are more me than I at times,
free spirited bird that soars and climbs.

Little Pieces

Every second on the clock
is needed to make up time.
Each jot and tittle,
brings the bell to chime.

Omit not one thought pure
when in its proper place,
to bestow upon the Master,
the richest kind of grace.

Each little piece is so important,
and all the parts are dear,
when all are joined together,
light from darkness may appear.

The Spirit seeks to be united,
with all around it living,
making life to grow and never end,
in the heart that's always giving.

The critic eyes the little pieces,
and does not see the whole.
What a waste of blessing,
if creation has no soul.

Little Snowflake

Have you ever watched a single snowflake
as it traveled to the ground,
spinning, winding, dancing,
its predestined journey falling down?

It doesn't go unnoticed
by the eye within the storm.
It's watched over patiently
by the Creator who gave it form.

Many look upon a forest
and cannot see the tree.
They miss the gift of knowing
a special kind of unity.

Little snowflake dance around me,
dainty winged fairy of the cold.
With frozen caress come warm me,
for soon I'll be old.

In the brevity of this life,
many opportunities pass us by,
if in our habit we fail to notice
the single snowflake in the sky.

Lonely Victor

How can one man's moment
select the words I use;
crowning me with sovereignty,
defeating other views?

Some other time will come
and release me from my crown,
when that man's moment
no longer is around.

Who then will be the victor
and sit upon the throne,
However long he rules there,
he will surely dwell alone.

Look Toward the Sky

We work together in the garden of God,
    there is much for us to do,
        pulling weeds and turning sod,
            beginning with each morning dew.

Once we uncover the plants,
    from the dampness of the night before,
        the sun will shine while nature chants,
            and each will rise to heaven's door.

We water as needed, each tender blade,
    speaking softly as we pass by,
        thanking the Master for all He has made,
            and we look upward toward the sky.

Man's Great Quest

The seeking shall be satisfied,
those asking will receive.
Each answer is a stepping stone,
in our struggle to believe.

The wealth of God is no man's treasure,
His standard not one could trace.
With selfish heart we all do measure,
Yet never scale God's gift of grace.

Man—The Limited Creature

Man cannot see beyond the skies,
he cannot prowl the deepest sea;
nor does he hear in the busyness
of his own soul,
the voice of God.

Yet he deems to judge
the least of things,
believing he understands,
his way from birth to sod.

To fashion any plan
of his own design,
while having no growing relationship
with the Creator,
I find this very odd.

Memories

An active mind
   is an interesting tool;
      edifying the wise,
         betraying the fool.

Fantasy, logic, reason,
   chaos, or rhyme;
      inhabit one home,
         living in three rooms of time.

What was, and is,
   and is to come;
      once inside the mind,
         can never be undone.

You cannot lose it,
   it's always there;
      forever within your reach,
         just beneath your hair.

Missed Opportunity

When you thought the worst of me,
    I was at my very best.
Though no witness defend me now,
    In time, I'll stand the test.
Who I am, what was really said,
    or what was done,
you never understood.
    You simply chose
to see the bad,
    and did not try
to look for good.

Misspoken Words

Words misspoken

come

like unexpected storms,

blowing us

not off course

but further out to see.

Morning Memories

Birds dancing in the wind,
head high above the grass.
Giving birth to flight and freedom,
with every hurried pass.

The morning mist now frozen,
upon both bough and limb.
Obscuring a clearer vision,
of nature's ordained hymn.

Crocus wave their solitary flower,
daffodils announcing spring.
Little squirrels shopping gaily,
over the ground go blanketing.

A doe bowing to nourish,
keeps a watchful eye.
Water lapping against the cattails,
in the teeming pond nearby.

"Take this picture of the morning,"
My sleepy eyes did say.
"And keep it in your heart,
for whenever you're away."

My Associates

I make my friends
    of the bent and broken,
and refrain from dwelling
    with the arrogant and outspoken.
I'll feed the poor
    and not dine with the rich,
make my home not a mansion
    but a prison or homeless niche.
There is peace to be found
    where men are most caring,
and the truth of their need
    is found in their sharing.

My Collection of Little Rocks

In my study on a shelf, I have a collection of little rocks.
These little rocks were given to me one at a time
by my daughter and granddaughters, crowned with golden locks.
Little girls humble and unknowing in their prime.

Holding your hand while dancing around your feet,
ignoring the conversation hovering above;
they pause a moment to pick a stone from the street.
To interrupt mankind's timing with a simple act of love.

A visit from an angel on any ordinary day,
bearing precious gifts, or so it would seem:
"This one's for you!" you hear, as they merrily dance away.
Gone off on another adventure, chasing another dream.

I bet there are a lot of little rocks lining pockets,
discarded thoughtfully, or lying somewhere on a shelf.
Touched by a child's hands becoming cherished amulets;
A most intimate act of sharing ones' self.

Tiny little gifts that were given from the heart,
paving the pathway that we walk upon,
with new eyes, not seeing the common, but great art,
building better days for all before we are done.

My Enemies

Marching always toward me,
in fierce array,
comes the many warriors,
seeking someone else to slay.

To do battle with my weakness,
and gather up my plunder,
consuming soul and body,
to feed their fiendish hunger.

But I've a special armor,
fashioned by a king,
I will be the victor,
over hordes with fearful sting.

This promise I've been given,
my faith in Christ will save.
He prevails through every battle,
and reigns beyond death and grave.

"Holy, Holy, Holy,
is the Lord God Almighty,
who was, and is, and is to come!"
(Revelation 4:8)

My Epitaph

To all of you,
    when I am through,
I beg you to forgive.

I've been immature,
    and ignorant,
but then, that's how we live.

We learn and grow,
    like lilies do
if given half the chance.

Perhaps some shade,
    I, too, have made,
while on my way to Heaven's dance.

My Great Regret

To all those who are dead and dear:
    I truly loved you when we were here.
Though love is a glass not always clear,
    without it life would be much more drear.

Now that time has passed for you and I,
    our space we did most brutify.
We failed to love and did not try;
    it was not meant for man to die.

This side of death will never tell,
    why we with pride did choose to dwell.
In sorrow holding firmly to our hell,
    surrendered soul for earthly shell.

Was there a gap we could not breach,
    some point together we could not reach?
Though life gave to both silence and speech,
    we could not draw and would not teach.

What once we shared while on this side,
    a longed for love was unapplied.
'Tis only death meant to divide,
    still I will trust the Greater Guide.

My Journey to Ezra

My master had given me another whipping, one I thought was most severe. He had judged I was headed in the wrong direction. Yet, the beating, served only to make my path more clear.

I determined to go where I was wanted. I ran fast and fearless to get away. No man would own my soul and my decisions would be my own. Without support or encouragement, I ran toward a light more brightened. Fearing not the dark of unknown days, I was drawn as if enlightened.

To make my world what I thought it should be, I made some friends fated same as me. Though wild creatures roamed everywhere about, through obstacle or opportunity we made our stand. We encouraged one another through the wilderness, until at last, we reached our promised land.

Not one person could give a reason, why we had stopped at such a forsaken place. But all knew, from the greatest to the least, where we belonged, we would soon embrace. Out of sorrow and shame were born praise and adoration, for each heart knew that, one day, we would become a great nation.

Dressed in rags, we appeared with our meager lot. Filled with hope and burdened with the many lessons we had learned, we found the cities had been pillaged and even the temples burned. Much of our time, though starved and weary, was given to trial and opposition. But each circumstance became a stone we placed, with care and determination.

Having gathered wood to strengthen the walls, each member grew more willing to do their share. Through joy or weeping, we wore our swords, to bless or curse any who beseech us there. We labored hard and we labored long. Sweat and tears became our slumber song.

Painstakingly crafted in humble reflection, the city, like a child, became our sacred connection. Poised for the finish, all gave a roar; no longer a slave, but each man a son, and all were equally proud when we were done.

"Make sacrifice, give offerings, and celebrate!" "The time for play, comes never too late!" Laughter and dancing breaking out in all the ranks. Even the smallest child mimicked our thanks. Old tired bones were renewed in baptized joy as a few brave hearts maintained a guarded employ.

Looking forward; we placed our few treasures on golden shelves, and with the city rebuilt, lay the tool upon ourselves.

We measured the cost not with engraved coin, but through lives given to labor and pain. Our faithful scribe, the pages turned, as we rededicated ourselves to the future we sought to gain.

A house restored, the people renewed, we dedicate it all to the King of kings, His Truth our beatitude.

My Life-Altering Prayer

I had walked a long way
to the solitary mountaintop.
A journey driven
by a hunger that would not stop.
The weight of my world
had become too heavy for me,
now grown to an age
where my eyes were open to see.
I had been walking in darkness,
finding no rest.
Only an act of God
could satisfy my quest.

Such a great distance
I needed to traverse;
overwhelmed with doubt and fear,
I had to reverse.
The long walk allowed me
to pour out some burdens along the way,
and helped to lighten the load
by the time I arrived to pray.
From heaven to this hill
I knew only God could transcend,
completely broken and humbled,
I was now prepared to attend.

Arriving I bowed
beside a timeworn stone,
where nothing created was higher,
just God and I alone.
Amid the confusion and turmoil,

I had come to find peace.
With my deepest groaning,
I laid out my fleece.
In the prayer that I thought
would take a great while,
quickly diminished was time
and erased every mile.

Firmly and faithfully
God took hold of my hand,
and led me as we strolled
over the beautiful land.
The Father who had bowed
to listen to this wayward child,
assured me of His total attention
even here in the wild.
A transformation began,
no more a beggar was I.
His glory revealed,
and I no longer asked: Why?

His Spirit embraced me
and in time we became one.
I had entered God's realm,
basking there with the Son.
The demons of ignorance
were all cast away.
A benefit unexpected
for someone needing to pray.
My mind renewed,
my complaints were all gone.
The glory of God on that hill
announced a new dawn.

There on the rock,
I stood straight and tall,

loudly singing the majesty of God
to angels and all.
With all my needs vanquished,
I called out His name,
filled with thanksgiving,
His praises proclaim.
As tears were streaming
down from my eyes,
I rejoiced looking upward
into the beautiful skies.

Then I heard His sweet voice
so tender and clear.
"Do you know how long my child
that I've waited here?
For you to look up,
standing on this very spot,
and give me credit
for all that you've got?"
The patience of God
now fell on my ears;
in that instant, I traveled
throughout all of my years.

I came here as one pleading,
but now praising God,
alone on the mountain
there in the sod.
Whatever argument
I came to defend,
I valued no longer
nor carnal attend.
Looking out at earth's beauty
I was reborn.
It was not just earth
but man God had bowed to adorn.

Though it was growing dark
and hours had passed by,
I was in no hurry
under the darkening sky.
Feasting on pure Love
comforted that all would be well,
I was transfused
with a strength that banishes hell.
Happily now I would return
to the valley below,
For faith not applied
leaves nothing to show.

Like twins birthed together:
His plan and my task.
I was given the message and ointment
for those that would ask.
The fellowship on the mountain,
this time of sharing,
will be known in the valley
if I am equally caring.
My prayer was answered,
He fulfilled all my needs,
And I know the prayer is not ended
until confirmed by my deeds.

Hallelujah! All Glory to God!

My Old Recliner

When evening comes and I find myself resting
in my favorite chair; hypnotized by the burning
embers with their man-made glare, I begin to
reflect on the course of my life.

Now that I'm finally retired; having been blessed
with many a year, I can reminisce freely while no one
is here, through chapter and verse of experiences rife.

The challenges I faced at every turn, opportunities
lost and lessons learned. I think about the motives by
which I was driven. So many decisions; too quickly
delivered, becoming debris someone else would be given.

I look upon the mantle, my legacy so firmly held.
Some trophies, the battles, portraits of a deep hurt or two.
Loved ones gone on before me, sadder times most
solemnly belled.

What fruit did I bear? What has made me what I've become?
While there is still time for confession and correction,
it is good to know—I am not done.

My Riddle

If I should ever long to be,

anyone other than who you see,

then give a warning and I shall cease.

and praise you highly for my release.

My Search to Find God

I saw God moving in Nature once,
    and I was sure it was He.
But as time and life passed by,
    I forgot His walk upon the sea.

Certain that I would find Him through Knowledge,
    I searched for all that I could know.
But the more I learned, the more I knew,
    not one jot would ever make me grow.

Then I tried Miracles and Signs,
    to take me to his throne.
Still, such evidence I could never control,
    and I remained alone.

Finally, weak and broken, I humbly bowed to pray,
    "Lord, I've looked everywhere. What Must I do?"
Then I heard Him say: "Be still, my child, and let me look."
    "I'm not lost. I'll come to you."

My Secrets

My secrets are very special to me,
little treasures that always glow,
Where no other eye can see,
there they dwell and never go.

Neither right nor wrong,
to judge me by.
Never shared with anyone,
rich or poor until I die.

Each risk or regret would sell a song,
forgotten only when they are told.
May each one keep me close to Him,
who keeps the end and has the gold.

Need a Ride?

I'm just standing here enjoying my meal,
    with nothing further planned at all.

My home allows the cold and rain to come in,
    but I'm pretty happy with my stall.

Things are quiet around here most of the time,
    though a lot of people come passing by.

If the news came for need of me,
    I'd be more than glad to give a try.

Though I'm small, I'm capable and strong,
    and ready for all kinds of work.

All you need to do, is loosen my cord,
    and give it a little jerk.

Just last week, a man came in,
    determined as he could be.

He walked by all the others,
    and came right up to me.

Boy was I proud when he looked at my owner,
    And said: "This is the one!"

I was to take a man all the way right into town,
    I believe they called him Son.

They put their coats upon my back and led me out,
    so he could climb aboard.

I never flinched a bit as I proudly climbed the hill,
    even though everyone was shouting: "This man is the Lord!"

Nettie

Sometimes in the night when I awaken
with a poem stirring in my breast,
my cat comes creeping for my attention
and lies upon my chest.

"How can I get anything written?"
I ask her once more.
Then I place the pen and paper
beside me on the floor.

So little she asks
of my highly treasured time,
unaware of the presence
of an inspired rhyme.

There are a thousand thoughts
each begging to be held,
but she stretches forth her paw,
and with a touch to my chin,
we become a perfect weld.

Not

There are many things,
    that waste the years:
Words NOT said,
    that should be spoken.
Deeds NOT done,
    no lasting token.
Kindness NOT shared,
    a friendship broken.
Plants NOT grown.
    in soil unsoaken.
And void created
    where NOT was sown.

Only a Veteran Knows

I've worn the scars of an awful war,
the sights and sounds and smells
of life being taken in battle.

I've carried, each day, memories
that cling to me like rotting flies.
Always looking for some place to dispose
the horrid trash of my mind.

I've drained every bottle of fermented time,
and chased a thousand counterfeit fantasies
until my flesh lay shriveled and slain
and some misguided eulogy marked my grave.

What family I had has forsaken me,
gone too quickly, determined to forget
and make a new hope for what lies ahead.
Blamed for all that died I journey on.

My book of life shows only pictures
of the choices I have made,
while the consequences are recorded
in some album in another world.

Yet, I still cling to a faith
that was born in me before my memory began.
For some reason, I am called to carry on;
Somewhere out there, a voice is calling me to come back home.

Opportunities

Through the portals,

we grasp the sea.

Little openings

to great adventure.

Time is spaced,

not for our censure,

but to rap upon the door

of eternity.

Orbiting About

Some people grow up
    in a frigid world,
        where boundaries are set
            by prejudice and pride.
The way they conceive
    and believe
        are unlikely to change
            for freedom to think has died.
They suppose and suspect
    that things different are wrong.
        Such great energy they expend
            advocating their view.
Like gravity, they hold things down,
    seeking to conform all to one globe,
        ever resisting the day
            when something new finally breaks through.

Our Furry Children

My Yorkie and my Schnauzer,
both sleep in my bed.
Lounging expectedly between me,
and the wife that I wed.
Guards of the night?
There be no such chore.
So soundly they sleep,
and unashamedly snore.
I've even slept poorly,
for their comfort and rest.
Loving both differently.
and never one best.
Dolly the lady,
and Kizer the man,
love unconditional,
all part of God's plan.
We gladly pay,
whatever the cost,
for their care and comfort,
just pray one never gets lost.

Part-Time God

Is God only to be loved

part of the time?

Should He be loved by just a few?

It seems that He deserves

a word from everyone,

and not just one or two.

Reach out and take the hand

of someone else that cares.

Thank God in harmony,

for all the things He shares.

Plagiarism

I've never copied

any man's work.

But if our words

are matched.

Any thoughts found

I'm sure,

were most cleverly hatched.

Play It for the Mountains

One day I want to go high up into the mountains,
to a place far away and hard to reach.
Perhaps a little cleft within the rocks,
or a place where God has carved a little breach.

When I find that special secluded place
where beauty spans as far as the eye can see,
I will sit in nature's chair with my pen in hand,
and compose a symphony.

Without a judge to rule my thoughts,
or anyone to silence my timid heart;
my words will be selected most prayerfully,
as I paint my work of art.

Each note will pour from my very soul;
so long awaited, this chore I'll gladly do.
Then I will stand and sing it just for the mountains,
without a pause until I am through.

The melody and words will come,
their journey through tears of praise;
dedicated to God—Who made each lovely leaf,
in these hills where I was raised.

Poetry Is Not Dead

Poetry is not dead,
    I did not see it die.
There will always be poetry,
    in never-ending supply.
From within the very soul of man,
    flows a river throughout time,
binding two hearts in sacred love,
    as earth and heaven rhyme.

Prison

Some people are imprisoned,
    for a cause and not a crime;
Their sentence often more severe,
    than many doing time.

Even a poor man whose life is pure,
    lives on the begging side of pride;
while a rich man roams freely,
    and in his haste won't be denied.

An ignorant man is bound in his folly,
    he alone is the keeper of the key;
but a wise man dwells in freedom,
    wherever he might be.

If you find yourself a captive,
    bound alone in hades cell;
seek no other prison,
    until the last has taught you well.

The bars are slick and polished,
    by the sweat of those gone before;
but for those who in life are learning,
    each cell is an open door.

Psalm 86:15

The Longest Verse in the Bible

God has taken you from where you WERE,

and brought you HERE,

to have you THERE!

"But you, O Lord, are a compassionate and gracious God, slow to anger, abounding in love and faithfulness."

Psalm 131

I no longer look down,
    from the heights where I used to dwell,
        pride, scorn, disdain, and contempt,
            have ripped open this earthly shell.

In bold blindness, I had judged others unworthy,
    and condemned them to failure,
        my upper room cluttered with the banquet,
            of my own selfish nature.

Promoting protests, originating opinions,
    and creating controversies, they are no more,
        the sin I once labored to develop,
            I now have learned to deplore.

I had even challenged creation,
    and matters far beyond my control,
        wonderful heights I had squandered,
            bringing doubt and death's door to my soul.

Calmed through years of misplaced passion,
    patiently lashed with Love's strong cord,
        I now dwell in green pastures beside still waters,
            and my hope is in the Lord.

Quotes From The Heart

How to know you are praying in the Spirit:
Simply pray until all that is unholy disappears!

Faith is the power by which any fate or
circumstance may be overcome!

We must ever seek to be forgiven,
and be always willing to forgive!

God has never granted man the freedom to worship!
Worship is where the Soul of God
and the Free Will of Man intertwine.

Evil is inherent in life,
but it cannot inherit it!

When it comes to writing:
I would rather see one stick of dynamite
on a page, than a bunch of little firecrackers!

Poetry, whether frail or sound,
is the greatest challenge I've ever found!

Dabble in the deviant
if you will,
be devoted to the Divine
you must!

A fool is a person highly educated in ignorance!

You can either spend your life
feeling sorry for yourself,
or your life can be spent
on the sorrow of others!

The greatest gift I can give my wife,
is to live each day knowing
that I absolutely adore her!

Humility—is being the least, and becoming the best!

I like the sound of rain,
it is the sound of forgiveness!

To fulfill faith,
we must allow fear.
For faith overcomes fear,
when we are closest to God!

From out of the darkness of fear, our faith is born.

A poet writes words,
and leaves them on pages,
when readers respond,
they fashion the ages!

"perspective" is how far we see here on earth.
"purespective" is how far we will see in Heaven!

Rain in the Mountains

By the thousands, the tiny warriors came,
their battle roar growing louder with each step.
All earth trembled as their thirsty feet met the ground;
shiny helmeted minions with their medaled breasts,
gluttonous victors honored throughout the past.

They brandish weapons of the best maker's design;
crowded conquerors spilling forth with little remorse,
unleashing judgment in a bloodletting bath.
Pouring over the wounded; the landscape changes,
they are too numerous to be defied; too loud their cannons blast.

Lightning streaks the sky as the drummers lead the way.
"Leave not one eye drying, there must be no retreat."
All fought with sacrificial devotion, knowing home was far behind.
The rainbow comes tomorrow,
the smell of victory is on the rise.

At the battle's end, there is a smoke that hovers,
a sudden quiet stills the soul.
The smell in the air is somehow clean again,
the clouds that were so dark have moved away,
and the sun has pierced the skies.

Rainbow

The rainbow marks a promise,
    God's honor written in the sky.
A hidden emerald nestled in the clouds,
    where angels go circling by.
From Creator to all creation,
    travels each celestial bow.
Always forward into the future,
    shining brightly as they go.
Praise God who would share such beauty,
    crossing His heart to spare the world,
Reaching into each soul of man,
    with a tiny bow unfurled.

Raping the Vineyard

Uninspired poets go trampling throughout the vineyard,
painting the virgin vines with their broken brushes.
Creating images that bear fake and artificial fruit,
not one ripening in its appointed time.
Drinking contaminated wine the crowd grows intoxicated,
while those who piped would not themselves dance.
Life flees before the butterfly lights,
the cold frost of winter approaches.

Rotting paper offers no salvation,
Untried the Word gives no direction.
Disfigured and diminished is the shepherd.
Surely the sheep will scatter.
The ark remains veiled.
The true wine yet to be tasted.
Life flees before the butterfly lights,
the cold frost of winter approaches.

Were it not for mercy, who would waken,
out of control this shaken sphere?
Those choosing too early their own dying,
born a bit naive have ceased trying to survive.
It is not for our sake we are living,
giving takes an endless toll.
Life flees before the butterfly lights,
The cold frost of winter approaches.

Reflections of a Vietnam Veteran

Little victims run asunder, scatter in the rain,
in the dark find a place to hide you,
both your sorrow and your pain.

Sandal-footed, wearing garb black as night,
even your clothing will betray you,
for they are coming in the night.

Roaring Phantoms swift as lightning passing by,
spitting out their fire and venom,
releasing hell before you die.

I'm overhead and watching, dropping flares to light their way,
there are questions I won't answer,
the price is just too high to pay.

Our futures were planned in yet another dawn,
where you would be erased and I would live,
to bear forever this canvas for me drawn.

Right or Wrong?

I've explored a bit and experimented some,
    but I haven't gotten into the habit of sin.
Like a child satisfying curiosity, I usually did,
    what I did without really joining in.

I tried to be careful and make very sure,
    that any punishment would be all mine.
Never wanting to harm or blame anyone,
    whenever I walked the darker line.

A little lie, some dishonest gain,
    a little cheating here and there.
I thought it couldn't be so bad or wrong,
    if it's being practiced almost everywhere.

But somehow I still wonder,
    how much the world would be improved,
if we all just decided to do what's right,
    and all the wrong had been removed.

Rise Up and Come Away

Has God tapped you on the shoulder,
could there be room for you in His plan?
Has He called you with love so tender,
this day designed before you began?
How awesome it would be,
if God spoke to you today:
> "My beloved one spake and said to me,
> Rise up, my love, and come away."
Everyone is invited to make this journey,
to gather around His throne.
For it has always been His will,
that none should walk alone.

(Verse from: Song of Solomon 2:10)

Roots

Always searching, always yearning,
    ever asking, never learning.
In a race of course aeration,
    running since their first creation,
hopeful digging in the dark.

Little snouts work hard at plowing,
    endless roads to nowhere going.
Without a plan are bent and twisting,
    so determined each stump resisting,
self-esteemed within their bark.

Above the earth goes someone common,
    advanced in form unlike a demon.
Will such a branch remain connected,
    or break away and be rejected,
to struggle with some man-made ark?

Whether roots or thinking man,
    both are guided by God's plan.
In the light or in the dark,
    God's love directs each arrow
to their mark.

Saying Good-Bye

Why does saying good-bye
    take so very long?
We would rather it be quickly over,
    with no accounting of the wrong.
All the penance could be handled,
    in the twinkle of an eye.
O' that our hearts would be bonded,
    here on earth before we die.
Many days we live in sorrow,
    watching as they gather into years.
No one should die without being forgiven,
    no one should shed this kind of tears.
We should plead before the highest court,
    to learn the right from wrong.
Together spending time in full confession,
    then saying good-bye wouldn't take so very long.

Scripture Trumps Satan

Satan will try to equal
    your joy in the Lord,
        with only concern
            for yourself.

Whenever he does
    just reach up high,
        and take your Bible
            down off the shelf.

Quote him some scripture
    and in a little while,
        fearful and anxious
            he will slither away.

He cannot stand
    the voice of God,
        that even he
            has to obey.

Secrets

Everyone should have a secret or two,
    a fantasy, a dream, or something they do.
A secret can bring a lot of joy when judged no harm,
    like blankets from the cold they help keep us warm.
Little privately chested treasures uncovering the glad,
    outshining the many negatives hurtful and sad.
Lying silent, coursing throughout the mind,
    our secrets hidden away where no one can find.
Each must be buried in a heart of good soil,
    where they shine for God's glory without any toil.
A good deed done, a sacrifice made, something positive said,
    a price for someone's joy you gladly paid.
Known only by the Master and you,
    dare yourself to have a special secret or two.

See Me!

I'm walking around in this body you see,
    but what's inside may not be me.
Look more deeply than you ever have before,
    do not pass by without opening a door.
There are riches to find and I'm willing to bet,
    you will never be the same once we've really met.
I've something to contribute as well as do you,
    created in the exchange something lasting and new.

We have joys to share and sorrows to bear,
    criticisms, judgments, opinions, and what we fear.
In no other time were each of us placed,
    just think of the unknowns that can be erased.
So many people pass by without ever saying hello,
    and life is so short before we have to go.
Somewhere in eternity we may meet again,
    and isn't eternity the meeting of a friend?

Seeing with God's Eyes

To God each flower is a bouquet of beauty,
    each day born tomorrows joy.
He sees with so much compassion,
    willing to redeem what we destroy.
Even the soul that goes astray,
    is patiently watched by God,
        in a very special way.
He sees the smallest offering,
    and knows all that we possess.
No child is ever forbidden,
    no one too bad to caress.
He sees the heart and looks on the soul,
    and when all seems to fall apart,
        He is there to make us whole.
God's eyes fill up with beauty,
    though Unseen, He sees us well.
Through Christ, God sees His glory,
    the image of the invisible God, Immanuel!

(Thought from Colossians 1:15)

Seeking the Pure

Help me, Father:
To clean the cup of my communion,
and bring my best to every union.
Let not the light that in me shines,
hold on to dark and carnal vines.
Forgive my greed that grew so viral,
and grant me grace to bear each trial.
When I lie down to rest in sleep,
may my soul be one you choose to keep.

Separation

I don't like separation,
it makes me very sad.
There is not one good thing to say about it,
it's negative, depressing, and terribly bad.
To come apart, be severed, and disconnected,
takes away from the purposed whole.
Separation forms an incompleteness,
that tears apart a sacred soul.
It is an evil intrusion upon God's sanctuary,
a trespassing sly and slithering fiend.
Obsessed with the task of turning,
a beautiful beginning into an ugly end.
Who can bear its strength,
once sin has made its mark?
shrouded in tattered rags mocking glory
leaving stumbling blocks in the dark.
Waving the banner of death arrogantly,
at the end of every life,
this power, this principality, whose dominion
knows nothing of eternal life.
It breaks down friendships, marriages,
families, partnerships, and causes wars.
Hospitals in every nation,
are filled with separation's scars.
Yet, though the pain of separation seems forever;
this unbearable burning in the heart,
we must keep faith for morning comes,
when darkness and weeping part.
Restoration and reunion have been promised,
the kind only a Messiah can bring.
Even now the sound approaches:
I hear from Heaven, the sound of praises ring.

Shapes in the Clouds

Thy nose is red
Ye puff-ed cloud.
Thee looks about,
who boasts so proud.
Dost thou not know,
thy fleeting span,
ordained of God,
unknown to man?
The words that shaped
and fellowed thee,
move through space and time,
but never flee.

Sign Searchers and Miracle Workers

Sign searchers and miracle workers;
    God bless them every one,
if they are truly sent from God,
    to do the same work that He has done.

We all need to be reminded,
    as we run the race toward the goal,
a lot of folks could use their healing,
    to keep their bodies tuned to soul.

But, even Jesus, avoided these means,
    when misguided people sought to show the Way.
It was FAITH He knew they needed,
    if they were ever going to stay.

Simultaneous Combustion

Any new thought is not pondered

by one man alone.

It springs forth simultaneously upon

the lips of many men.

while we may be secluded

in our own designs,

destiny around our kindred soul entwines.

Sin and Grace

The stillness of the morning cannot be stolen.
it is sacred to the Lord.
As man wakes to interrupt the silence,
he bends the bands of Heaven's cord.
With the life that man is given,
he must make a faithful run.
that all may dwell in lovingkindness,
where the robe of God is spun.

Sitting on My Porch

Little droplet on a leaf,
how far you've come to bring me cheer.
Before you dry or become absorbed,
I make a wish you prosper here.

I've come for rest and solitude,
there is much to be said for slowing down.
To renew oneself in blissful thought,
I crave no greater crown.

It's odd that I have spied your perch,
or that you should impress me so.
But time and chance have planted you there,
and I alone will ever know.

Shall I fathom out the mystery,
that you and I have formed this bond?
Was it ordained that I choose this chair,
and you through miles have dropped upon that frond?

I commune with you remaining silent and still,
for much is said that none can hear.
The voice of God that reaches both,
is both now and forever clear.

Though I must retire and go to bed,
I confess a little grief,
The body wears before the soul,
little droplet on a leaf.

Sometimes God Cries

The congregation was seated,
and with anticipation quieted down.
The music had placed a robe upon the Lord,
and now would come the crown.

The preacher walked toward the pulpit,
clutching a Bible in his hand.
Silent moments passed by,
the people prepared for praise or reprimand.

Had someone died in the community;
what caused his look of grief and pain?
Gone was his usual approach with laughter,
now overwhelmed with emotion he could not explain.

Each member braced for the unexpected,
hoping their faithful leader would carry on.
Huge teardrops fell from his eyes,
as though coming from beyond.

He raised a hand above his head,
as if to signify control.
With the Bible in his other hand,
he looked like Moses with a scroll.

Finally, he uttered three simple words,
just bold enough that all could hear,
His message was from God's own heart,
spoken loud and clear:

"Sometimes… God… cries!" he mourned,
and then he fell to his knees and wept.
Finished was the sermon, and everyone arose,
unspoken, the invitation, that each one could accept.

With an electrifying silence,
penetrating every timeworn pew,
it was as if all the angels in heaven bowed down,
to see what the crowd would do.

Erring and penitent, the sorrowing children came,
joining the pastor at the altar and bowed to pray.
The day after the Newtown Elementary School Massacre,
They, too, could not bear what God was feeling that day.

Starting Over

Of all the stars in the sky,

there is one that caught my eye.

Each time I look out into the night,

You are there, shining bright.

That sweet glow from within your heart,

has given me a complete new start.

Now I'll laugh, and love, and live again,

Reborn, I'll not look back to where I've been.

Suppose You Were God

Suppose you were God,
and made yourself a world.
In it you placed a garden,
and made little creatures to roam about.

Watching them awaken;
as each new day unfurled,
how long would you be happy,
watching them go in and out?

Suppose you still had a longing,
for someone to share your joy.
To know what you were thinking,
and how you feel inside.

They could help you tend your garden,
and learn how to build and not destroy.
Would you give them total freedom,
if you knew you would be denied?

If they took away everything,
and left you all alone,
would you rise up in anger,
wanting to start all over in another place?

Or would you still pour out your love,
like a river from your throne,
offer them a second chance.
and wisely call it Grace?

Sweat

There are only three times in the Bible where the word "sweat" is mentioned. There is a great message for us here. Read these scriptures and perhaps you will also enjoy my poem.

Sweat (1)
Genesis 3:19

Bread you eat
   in sorrow and toil,
      you would not take
         from purest soil.

The watered garden
   from which you came,
      forever banished
         will be your claim.

Sin is written
   upon thy face,
      thy legacy given
         to all your race.

Thorns and thistles
   shall be your curse,
      with sweat forever
         to fill your purse.

Drops of blood
   drawn in sorrow,
      to cleanse a soul
         you cannot borrow.

Sleep your rest
  in lifeless dust,
    for sake of truth
      you would not trust.

Sweat (2)
Ezekiel 44:18

Who comes to God
  to rid mankind,
    the ageless curse
      not one can find.

Even the priest
  ordained to pray,
    if wearing wool
      is turned away.

My house shall be
  a house of prayer,
    forbid the priest
      that does not care.

The Word of God
  no idle threat,
    reveals the heart
      with sin-filled sweat.

Sin may not enter
  the inner court,
    where good and bad
      God's sword doth sort.

The Law is harsh
  and so it stands,
    if cursed ground is tilled
      with sweating hands.

Sweat (3)
Luke 22:44

Through love one came
   to break the seal,
      and through His name
      all nations heal.

The Great High Priest
   The Worthy Lamb,
      God in Flesh
         The Great I AM.

In the garden
   where He prayed,
      our sweat was washed
         in His own blood.

The curse removed
   from all mankind,
      one act of love
         one life resigned.

Each has a choice
   to sweat or bleed,
      to gather spoil
         or fill a need.

The Door is open
   a Way is made,
      when Grace was given
         our debt was paid.

Symphony of Feelings

If feelings were metered out in music,
    what tune would you play?
Who would listen in this grand auditorium,
    to what you had to say?
Would the music soothe and soften,
    some heart needing mending.
Might some pain be diminished,
    or just more condescending.
We need a little symphony,
    soaring melodically through the air,
Each note plucking away,
    our pain with tender care.
There are so many instruments,
    given to man to play.
And each could bear such beauty,
    simply breathed upon today.
Our grandest talent,
    might be to listen to another's sound,
where gathering all their feelings,
    we loosen the torment bound.
Perhaps to encourage others,
    with the cleansing call to praise,
such a symphony of feelings,
    to our Creator could we raise.

Tea Cup Philosophy

Tea that keeps on pouring,

will overfill a cup.

But if another is placed beneath it,

all the remnants are gathered up.

Love is a bit like tea,

pouring, running over, and splattered all about;

though many may question,

loves origin before the spout.

How good it would be,

if we allowed our love to spill over,

into one another's cup;

adding a drip or two here and there,

until each cup was full and sharing,

and any difference would disappear.

Teach Me to Pray
(Mark 14:32–42)

Prepare for me,
    a place to sit.
For someone's care,
    I must not quit.
May I not depart,
    cause me to stay.
For someone's care,
    this price I pay.
Teach me to pray,
    and not to sleep.
For someone's care,
    this watch I keep.
When all is done,
    and help assured.
I will bow my head,
    and thank you, Lord.

Teach Us to Pray

I've never been very good at prayer;
but not for lack of trying or because I didn't care.
It's hard getting down on my knees in some dark place,
and talk to someone unseen and hope for grace.

Must I be broken or overwhelmed with fear,
I don't see a rock bottom anywhere in here.
I need to hurry, I have so much to do;
talk about strange, this is altogether new.

This is definitely not my comfort zone;
what if someone should hear me in this closet all alone?
There has to be a better way,
for telling God what He already knows I'll say.

I wish I had a card or something to read,
Please, Jesus, hurry up and satisfy my need.
Well I've got to go, I think I'm done.
Yes, my phone is ringing, I've got to run!

Thank God for Those Who Pray for You

There are people praying for you,
    even when you don't know.
Lifting up your name to God,
    watering precious seed He means to grow.

In times of sickness, pain, or sorrow,
    through each trial and all the strife,
God sends His angels to guard with prayer,
    each and every precious life.

Those who humbly bow to pray,
    and do the best they can.
Honored to share your suffering,
    giving thanks for God's eternal plan.

Comforted are they through intimate caring,
    your name they bear up to His throne.
The only reward they ever seek,
    is for you to know you're not alone.

The All Inclusive God

There is no "me,"

There is no "I."

God made it that way,

and I don't know why:

> "OUR Father which art in Heaven,
> Give US this day
> OUR daily bread.
> And forgive US OUR debts,
> As WE forgive OUR debtors.
> And lead US not into temptation,
> but deliver US from evil:"

  (Matthew 7)
From the very beginning,

  He said it the same,

He created US all,

  and gave US our name:

> "Let US make man in OUR image,
> after OUR likeness:
> and let THEM have dominion."
>   (Genesis 1)

He created THEM,

    He blessed THEM, each with his brother.

Oh, Father! Now I understand.

    Our blessings must come through one another.

The Art of Thinking

Thinking, like a heartbeat, is the pulsing of the mind,
an untamed and unfettered worthless child.
But with proper training, no man need be blind,
running amuck, frantic, and wild.

Thinking is the scale upon which we weigh each bill,
for each thought places a value on what we prefer.
It is the land of choice for those born of free will,
where no one can be forced his thoughts to defer.

Thinking allows us the opportunity to wander,
to speculate, carefully consider, and even doubt;
to consider our options, to reason, and ponder,
and in the face of uncertainty figure things out.

The thinking of a thoughtful man is articulate conception,
though many judgments are made good and bad.
A world without thought would be a deception,
for God gave man imagination to make him glad.

The Brightest Light

There are so many different religions in the world today,
teaching men how to worship, how to behave, and how to pray.

If we could just get together, sharing all that we know,
would so many be misguided believing things that aren't so?

To assert that one's faith is superior can be divisive and blind,
for love that is not boastful is the most precious kind.

It's not where you worship or the day that you choose;
but, forsaking all to honor God, you gain through what you lose.

That's what God did when He sent us His only Son.
Pouring out all His love is more than all the others have done.

There are laws and rules a plenty made by man to obey,
but these were never meant to come between us and get in our way.

To empty oneself for the sake of mankind here upon this earth,
demands all the love you have and shows your truest worth.

When at the end, totally unselfish and depleted you lie down,
if for the glory of God you've acted, be assured there is a crown.

The Can Man

"Don't throw that away!" "Save it for the can man."
"It's time for him to be coming by."

We seldom exchange a word when he comes for cans,
but then, I guess he's just shy.

That long flowing beard and well-worn hat; his farmer overalls
and long-sleeved shirt must help to protect him from the bugs,
and all the roadside dirt.

Ever humble, slightly bent, with that slow gaited walk,
the stories his shoes could tell, if only they could talk.

I found him picking up drink cans from the side of the road,
and stopped by to say: "If you come by the house,
I may be able to add a little to your load."

Now he comes by faithfully, once a month,
to gather the bags of cans I've placed outside.

As his paint-chipped car slips quietly down my drive,
I pause to honor the can man who works so dignified.

The Coins I Carry

I carry little coins of thought in my mind,
blowing about irresponsibly like untamed wind.
It remains unknown where these I find,
Little coins, two sided; used to buy, sell, or lend:

        deceit / truth,
        sorrow / joy,
        weakness / strength,
        loneliness / fellowship,
        doubt / faith,
        hatred / love,
        fear / reward,
        foolishness / wisdom,
        taking / giving,
        strife / peace,
        death / life

These I disperse when a battle is fought,
shaping my character into saint or fool.
A simple coin toss determines what I have bought,
and reveals whether I have learned to serve or rule.

The Doctor's Visit

I finally went to a dermatologist,
first time I had been.
The parking lot was very full,
cars were parked from here to then.

'WAIT HERE FOR NEXT ATTENDANT'
The sign greeted me when I walked in.
Forms were completed, cards all copied,
a smile submitted, I returned one with a grin.

Following instructions, I chose a random seat,
and waited for my call.
People popping up and down,
two TVs blaring on the wall.

Not a bad place to work, I thought;
neat and clean, this room without a hall.
Lots of help, and friendly, too.
caring servants, healing Concord's sprawl.

My name was called and I proceeded;
of course, I offered a little prayer.
Then I was guided to the room of:
"Take off your clothes and leave on your underwear."

I thought it strange but I complied,
I just came to check that spot behind my ear.
But there I was in my little gown,
trying to cover up my derriere.

Finally, the lady doctor came in,
and I knew my choice hadn't been wrong.
With thoroughness and skill she looked,
my dermal inspection proceeding along.

Like a carousel I turned, bravely as I could,
making conversation about the art on the wall.
Then she said: "I'm going to spray a place or two."
"It shouldn't hurt very much at all."

Biopsies were recommended just to be safe,
and soon I began to feel assured.
There is something about going to the doctor,
that makes you feel already cured.

"I will know in just a few days," she said.
"But for now, everything is looking great."
As I dressed, I did so thankfully,
knowing God watches over those who wait.

The Early Hours

Sometimes I find myself singing
some sweet hymn whenever I awaken.
I'm always thankful for the morning joy,
when my soul is so gently shaken.

These early hours are good for prayer
and I love a good old psalm.
God's Word comforts me as I lie still,
it's always been my healing balm.

Very soon the day will be filled,
and busy I will be.
Please, dear Lord, give me this time,
to have a little talk with Thee.

Let me just pray a prayer of praise,
and send me on my way.
Guide me, Lord, in everything I do,
and in every word I say.

This world is blessed in so many ways,
with all the Laws you put in place.
You knew before we came along,
that we would also need your Grace.

I love you, Lord, and thanks again,
for we know we are not alone.
Keep us in your will, O Lord,
that we all may gather around your throne.

The Filly and the Mule

He's been called stupid, foolish, stubborn, and worse,
though large and strong and more sure-footed than any horse.

Rising up early, harnessed with the morning dew,
the fields he's plowed have fed more than just a few.

Unlikely to be praised because he wasn't built for show,
there's hardly any load he's unable to tow.

She, on the other hand, stands proudly with her charm,
lively and high-spirited, not bred to work any farm.

Attention she seeks, like dry ground thirsting for rain,
running wild, unbridled, and free in her domain.

Her place is secure and so is her nest,
as long as she thrills with her beauty and zest.

Many a man and woman are like these two,
each have their own calling and special work to do,

Together they can make things good and strong,
as long as they go where they each belong.

Animals don't seem to bother and worry or fuss,
or make a big issue about equality like us.

To be equal is not to claim the same duty or pay,
but to share unique gifts, helping one another along the way.

The First Twins

Both were created when time began,
as places for homes for the good and bad man.
Priests came to one and pagans the other,
entered by sacrifice or slaying a brother.
In the freedom of choosing each man is bidden,
a promised mansion or an underworld hidden.
When the final war rages, whose house is most full,
where one owner is bound, and the other will rule?
Each knee is bowed and each tongue will tell,
which is better, Heaven or Hell.

The Friend Ship

When you needed me, was I strong,
did my gentle voice become your sail?
Each time it was I who was wrong,
did I try next time not to fail?
Was I ever way too proud,
that you never saw me bent and bowed?
When rough waters overtook my crew,
did I lash the cargo protecting you?
Did I share in my quarters my deepest thought,
and keep to myself harsh words I ought?
Was wealth in the hold with heart to give it away,
the anchor lowered to deliver poverties pay?
Did my words comfort and give you aid,
cheering you like ale with what I said?
Did you believe when I stood for truth,
setting a course to renew your youth?
Was I bold, but a little meek,
and just the right amount of weak?
Whenever you were apart from me,
did you realize how much I wished to be,
a friend to trust, a ship that sailed?
If so, then I will know, I haven't failed.

The Gardener
(John 20:11–18)

He tended the Garden,
    always keeping it green.
His trade mistaken;
    turning sod to reveal the unseen.

The sacrifice cross disfigured,
    now winnowed the field.
With a word spoken soft and gentle,
    he compelled her to yield.

Unprepared, for it was morning,
    she pleaded with him to know:
"Would you lay away the Master?"
    "Show me His rest, and quickly I will go."

Determined to pay homage,
    though all the others had gone,
for his care to the end,
    she had been faithfully drawn.

Like an arrow to her heart;
    one glance and one word,
her name He called,
    her name she heard.

It was all she needed,
    for then she knew.
She had been illumined by a gardener,
    in Messianic debut.

The Great Physician

Your body is the Garden,
one you must not defile.
Once sin has come to do its damage,
The soul is carried through the trial.
Pardon comes to those who seek it,
and with forgiveness comes relief.
Still forever the body labors,
'till Jesus comes to heal our grief.

The Great Recession of 2008

A bad economy? Why, there's no such thing.
Just misspent money, misguided motives, and
manipulating manager's finagling.

Economy by itself cannot be either good or bad.
It takes human involvement to determine
whose been had.

Lying, trickery, cunning, and deceit,
can outrun any paperwork,
and they offer no receipt.

Raising taxes or reducing spending,
a lobbied lie or untold truth,
why not just stop the morality bending.

We may graph and scale our course,
but for real growth to occur,
we just need to trace the problem to its source.

The Hourglass

Not for novelty, curiosity, or coin were you formed,
your duty is simply spilling the sands that God has warmed.

The narrow canal through which you rain,
carefully caresses each measured grain.

In a trickle you run from one place to another,
your glory revealed on the back of a brother.

Coming and going, pouring and flowing,
without offspring, yet constantly growing.

Time is remembered, spent, or saved to be weathered,
but you have provided a way for time to be measured.

Inevitable thought has fashioned your journey through time.
Perhaps there is more yet to be learned in this pouring paradigm.

The Human Spirit

Life sometimes is a mystery, a challenge to be met.
some people are rich and some are poor, never getting out of debt.

Some are weak and some are strong, and all will question why.
Life may be brief, or very long but in the end, we all must die.

Can we change the things that are, who takes the time to care?
Are we left with just a little hope, decaying in despair.

Fate bears down on everyone, still faith comes shining through.
The human spirit reaches up to God, who has a better view.

The Interstate!

How I long for a peaceful drive on the Interstate,
with new thoughts to feed upon and meditate.
As I shift my mind into gear and let go of the past,
I'm in no particular hurry, no desire to go fast.
I long for a nice ride just cruising along,
maybe turn on the radio and find a favorite song.
Upward I go as I enter the ramp,
just my wheels and me, the interstate tramp.
I will cherish the mental record of all that I see,
relax and refresh, what a day this will be.
Leaving all the hurried world behind,
let's just see now what I find:

   blinking white dashes,
     forbid those centerline crashes,
       reflecting pad protection,
         better roads promised next election,
           EXIT signs so compelling,
             cars compacted with kids yelling,
           emergency lanes,
          wrecker cranes,
            patrol cars looking for liquors,
           outdated inspection stickers,
          safety belts secure,
            air bags working for sure,
          out of state tags,
          insurance lags,
         rubbernecking,
           GPS and radar tracking,
          dip in the road,
            wide and overweight load,

brakes lit up like ornaments,
bright lights creating squints,
   long straights and sharp curves,
   a sleepy driver swerves,
     barricades,
     short visor shades,
        passing an occasional antique,
        rebuilt to match their peak,
          blackened tar patches,
          traffic jams in batches,
            roadwork ahead,
            roadkill squashed and dead,
              overpasses,
              another merger of chassis,
              mile marker signs,
              littering fines,
                cruise control,
                approaching toll,
                  flagmen to pity,
                  cars nasty and gritty,
                    orange and white cones,
                    turnpike zones,
                      unwelcome detour ahead,
                      no telling where we'll be led.
                      "Deliver me now!
                      O My God! There's a cow!"

Please let me off and I'll behave!
I'm not really cut out to be an Interstate slave!

The Language of God

How and when was it decided

that Word and Deed be divided?

Let each expose his mortal shame

who tries to live with just a name.

No place exists where one may tarry,

unless it be the cemetery.

The Little Cross

I found the little cross
    lying on the floor,
and wondered how it got there,
    didn't you want it anymore?

It meant so much to me
    when I placed it in your hands.
The shiny cross I carried,
    to many distant lands.

It's not the metal it's made of
    that gives it its worth.
Nor the shape it has taken,
    like no other here on earth.

It was chosen by someone long ago
    to symbolize how love came to die,
and to give our lives greater meaning,
    whenever we ask why.

Just a little treasure
    I wanted to pass along.
A part of me no one else would have,
    to remind you how I lived,
and now, to where I am gone.

The Lord's Friend

It does not matter the state of one's health,
nor does life come through the power of wealth.
To be loving and kind as one needs to be,
will grant you God's friendship throughout eternity.

Argue, complain, fuss if you must,
but only let God know your disgust.
He can handle anything you dish out,
though Hell you enter and Heaven you doubt.

With God as your friend; your companion each day,
others you love might also discover the Way.
Let faith guide you; in loyalty be true,
and with childlike trust, you'll see things anew.

When behaving like God becomes your best trait,
no fear can pierce the place where you wait.
Not even reward do you claim for your own,
satisfied to praise God upon His throne.

The Mirror

Look into the mirror and see,
past, present, and future in your eyes.
Is it your best friend or worst enemy?
Everything you think, say, or do, all before you lies.

What's become of the seed of your birth?
No other is there to take the blame,
lest their image should appear,
where now stands the one in pride or shame.

Who was it that silenced the truth in you,
quenching any hope for greater health?
Who came along and hid your skills,
taking away your potential and your wealth?

The face of blame is hardly ever seen,
yet many lives were ruined by this foe.
Accepting responsibility for personal deeds,
is necessary if we are going to grow.

The greatest task you will ever face,
will be to rise victorious in spite of strife,
to overcome the mistakes you made,
and alter the course of your own life.

The Mystery of Christ

The food we eat is quickly consumed,
according to the habit of each one fed.
Yet, from bird, to fish, and on to man,
all energy comes from the same morsel of Bread.

How is it that each one lies down and falls asleep,
when so many storms pass their way;
to simply bathe their cares in some doubtful deep,
while God prepares another day?

Mysteries are kept hidden for ages;
mountains of unknown at their peak.
Yet, a Way is made before we arrive,
and a Word is given before we speak.

Every act of faithful servitude,
reveals the glory and richness of God's plan.
Encouraged in heart and united in love,
the mystery is understood by man.

The doubts are dissolved when we obey,
faith and hope are joined as one.
All the treasures of wisdom and knowledge,
are given through Christ, God's only Son.

(Inspiration from: Colossians 1 and 2)

The Naked Soul

The soul that bares itself

    and risks being seen naked

        threads the robes

            of tomorrow's clothing.

The People We Pass By

Have you any idea where I was, when I wrote these lines?
I could have been reclining in front of a warm fireplace,
watching the sparks dance away like seconds on a clock,
with the family in bed, a dog at my feet, and I, chasing another dream.

Or, I could have been lying on a hard bench in some park,
beneath a streetlight dimmed by winter's cold storm,
with no home to go to or anyone there to greet me.
My writing pad; the backside of a discarded food wrapper,
this broken pencil, one of my few worldly treasures.

Perhaps in a hospital bed with chemo zapping the last dregs
of my life as the night shift saunters sleepily past my door.
This could be my last will and testament—my benediction.
Do you know what it's like to be leaving for good,
into some unknown with only silence at your side?

Dreaming, abandoned, or chronically ill,
do you know what I was really feeling inside?
Did you know that we were very close though we never met?
Every day investments are made by people all over the world,
but in our haste, we fail to profit where there is greatest gain.

"Excuse me!" I said as you hurriedly passed by.
Quickly erased, I became unnecessary and unknown.
In the absence of our knowing, we demean our greater cause.
Did you lose anything of value by never getting to know me?
In your blindness, did you ever come to see the light?

The Pier

I am standing here like a child,
    looking out at this big old pier:
"Huge sticks of wood,
    who put you here?"

"Who played in this water,
    digging out the holes;
laying out the foundation,
    and placing in these poles?"

Such great power in the ocean,
    water splashing side to side;
echoes of creations timing,
    with each new rising tide.

I hear the muffled roar of the waves,
    lapping at the wet sandy beach;
washing the little collectible houses,
    with every repeated reach.

At the base of each pillar,
    encrusted seaweed and fishermen's hooks.
My camera eye quick to focus,
    on sea creatures returning looks.

The sound of people scurrying along,
    with their floppity sandpapered feet;
would fill a treasure chest of memories,
    for a journey they will surely repeat.

These simple sights and sounds,
    the water merging with wood,
paints each one with a calm assurance,
    a timeless sense of peace and life is good.

The Pouting Poet

Laboring long, I searched for the flow,
saddened when the stream had dried,
like a child short of the goal,
disappointed and sullen, helpless I cried.

The desert barren before me,
leafless trees in the hot sun,
no wind blowing,
had the enemy won?

Craving for my mind to be fused,
by a power that finds each word its mate,
I stared at the page,
an empty hell, void certificate.

When the spirit for writing comes,
the drought yielding to a newborn will,
I dare not resist the thought,
that beckons my pad and quill.

Hastily, I'll loosen some words
and set them free,
then I will more content
and honored be.

From where is this power born,
this insane lust to exist,
that drives the writer to write,
a word no darkness can resist?

The Prayer Closet

Hope is nurtured in the womb of prayer,
where our requests are hidden from mankind.
Edited and delivered to God with care,
through a power no evil can bind.

Drawing each soul to God's great throne,
to attend like an angel where needed.
Sifting through as multitudes groan,
to find the spark that someone pleaded.

As God looks down from above,
drawn with listening ear and seeing eye,
in even the smallest prayer bathed in love,
He heals away the tears we cry.

Holy Spirit, please find us upon our knees,
as you fashion each feeble limb.
Then one day we might awaken and rise,
and with our prayers abide with Him.

The Pure in Heart

Why is it

that some people

feel

ugly and exposed

when they look

on something

naked and beautiful?

The Puzzle

He puzzled over the pieces before him,
drawing silently from the past.
Until the vision he remembered,
became a worthy cast.

Was it somewhere he had been,
or a place he wished to go?
Broken bits with contoured edges,
drew his interest sure and slow.

He played at the table like one searching.
content to be so driven.
Not one piece would be misplaced,
all would fit where they were given.

Life mattered most when came success,
and the revelation was known to all.
He had sculpted death to life once again,
the humble surgeon had heard the call.

The Three Motives

Lord, though I FEAR Thee,
may that not be my test.
Nor REWARD me with treasures,
to bring out my best,
Let LOVE be the door,
where entering I find perfect rest.

The Tree of Life

Those who fail to wonder cannot know,
the rooted tree from which they grow.
For buried beneath earth's crusty shelf,
lies the other half of each man's self.

Root or branch, we cannot flee,
for life was born of one lone tree.
A house conflicted is never whole;
nowhere in heaven dwells a divided soul.

How much escapes our primal cause,
when we enforce a prejudiced pause.
The banners we carry, the mantra we shout,
will never enable one blossom to sprout.

Protesting to defend one's priorities
grants no freedom and enables no growth.
No cost is worthy,
if in the journey opposition destroys both.

Both root and branch will be withered away,
and each new generation will reap what is sown.
Death offers no salvation nor gives one more day,
for each severed stem causes even nature to groan.

If there is to be hope each voice must be heard.
What we do here, will in heaven be done,
"They without us," or "we without them"
will only keep us detached from God's only Son.

The Unicorn and the Onion

Unicorn and Onion met one fine day,
on the road where many travel,
past the town of Happy Way.

With little in common they eyed one another,
"What are you doing here?"
each asked their brother.

Onion declared: "It was not by Fate,
and not by my choice,
that we have become the other's mate."

Then Unicorn spoke: "In all the annals of time,
we like puppets have been placed here,
to fit some gigantic rhyme."

"It must be Faith; a plan of a higher power."
"I shall choose to pass the test,
may this be my finest hour!"

"We are not victims nor captives in one cage,"
corrected Onion,
"we are just two words on the same page."

The Valley

One afternoon, in the mountains near our home,
my family and I were out just riding around,
when we happened to come upon a young artist,
with his easel and paints perched out over a valley,
painting nothing but mountains and trees and ground.

I thought it strange that he should be painting a scene
so common; a place that anyone could freely see.
There were no dilapidated old barns or houses,
no waterfalls, wildlife, or anything unique. "He will
never sell that picture!" I said assertively.

Perhaps he was one of those starving artists, a newbie,
with limitations he didn't fully understand.
So, I just continued driving on down the road while we
enjoyed our outing. We would find our own happy
place, one much more grand.

As time passed by, the kids grew up and went off to school.
My wife and I began to find time for leisure, shopping, and such.
On one particular occasion, in unanimous excitement, we stopped
at an old antique store. A favorite spot because of the history
and the prices weren't very much.

I found myself reading from a musty old book of poems shelved
beneath a single-pane window letting in far too little light.
Attracted to the treasure that I had found, I began to travel
down the winding lanes of word filled dreams. And then it
dawned on me: "That artist was right!"

It is the soul of the painter hungering for art to be born,
there where the gold is found, a gem to place in God's crown.
Far too many pass by, too busy to see, what never once caught the eye.
The artist had looked into heaven's door as I had done with books,
past scars and wounds and rags to view the Master's gown.

The 'Vangelist!

The lecture he gave them,
    was quite a spill.
Hurriedly, he had mounted the podium,
    bearing not one thought of ill.
Flailing about wildly,
    with his hands and arms,
convincing young and old,
    that he lacked any charms.
Turned loose like a madman,
    timed by the clock,
his only defense:
    "I stand on the Rock!"
A power much greater,
    commanded the floor,
and not one soul,
    moved for the door.
Most eloquent he spoke,
    unlike a fool,
with zeal to drive out demons,
    he wielded his well sharpened tool.
All listened in earnest,
    as he summoned each passage.
Who would claim the most souls,
    messenger or message?
The invitation would tell,
    how well the word was received,
if just one stood before God,
    and cried out: "I believe!"
Perspiring and exhausted,
    he wiped his brow,
as he heard the Father declare:
"That's enough for now."

The Word of God

The Word of God was not given
to be words resting on stone,
but placed in the soul
like seed to be sown.
God receives the glory
and His Word is revealed,
when deeds have sprouted
and fruit is abundant in each harvested field.

Thrown

Joseph was thrown into a kings prison,
and he became a great leader (Gen. 39:20).

    When suffering comes, do you,
    too quickly pray for release?

Shedrach, Meshach, and Abednego were thrown
into the fiery furnace,
where they met the Son of God (Dan. 3:25).

    With the burning flames all around,
    is there still faith that will not cease?

Daniel was thrown into the lion's den,
and the mouths of the lions were shut (Dan. 6:22).

    When in darkness where doubt seeks to devour,
    do you see the light increase?

Jonah was thrown into the raging sea,
and the sea grew calm (Jon. 1:15).

    When we enter our greatest storm,
    it is there the sea grows calm,
    and we can meet with Peace.

Time and Space

Robert Frost was living when I was born,
though we never met.
I might have learned a lot from him;
or lack of knowing me, might have been his debt.

He traveled freely much like me,
perhaps closely we might have passed.
Whose honor would the greater be,
what judge could stay the tribute cast?

How queer to think how close we were,
without exchanging a single word.
The birth of all that thought left vain,
might history weep for that not heard?

When death comes to take hold of me,
and I like he am gone,
perhaps we will together be,
beneath some tree on Heaven's lawn.

Tips for Prayer

When you go to God in prayer,
there are words you are bound to speak.
But consider that God may whisper,
when the noise all around has made you weak.

Do not sound religious,
or stretch a pious chord.
Remember He is not a genie,
watch what you are asking of the Lord.

First, confess the sin inside you,
If necessary, get on your knees.
Repent for all your failure,
He loves all honest pleas.

If there is a question you need to ask of God,
and a simple answer is all you seek,
be sure to approach Him with humility,
and show yourself to be a little meek.

Take some time to consider,
that you might be the answer to your request.
If so, then don't bother God with pouting,
just get up and go, complete the task and rest.

Don't talk to God like He owes you,
pray for the grace to hear His voice.
Hurry not, and when He answers,
when your Why? is gone, rejoice.

Never pray for small solutions,
when patching up mistakes and such.
Expect no signs or miracles,
faith doesn't grow through these very much.

In a thorough conversation,
never a question will remain.
If things get muddled while you are praying,
trust the Holy Spirit to explain.

If you have stepped out of your comfort zone,
and you are willing now to obey,
just offer up a word of thanksgiving,
and pray the prayer you need to pray.

To the Child in the Womb

Small child entombed while passing here
whose heart lies beating warm and secure,
you must wait for your time is not yet come.
Nourished in your protective home,
your day will greet you with a smile.

Each move disturbs the outside world,
you who long to be the next unfurled.
That solitary place in which you live,
unlike your next is all you have.
Just rest a little while.

Quickly, death occurs to all who leave,
entering this life, new breath must breathe.
Fear not in passing that darkened door,
you will pass by it but one time more,
until, home at last, your final mile.

The Old Writer

Should an old man write,

as a young man would?

Must he hurry his work,

before life passes on?

Can he recapture thoughts,

as he knows he should?

Before his ink is dry,

will he be gone?

Too Shy to Sing

There is a song in me

    longing to come out.

But, if I sing it,

    you'll know what I'm about.

Somehow, you'll know where I hurt,

    how I feel, and where I go to hide.

I risk a high cost of rejection,

    even the banishment of pride.

The tune may bore you,

    and I may be off-key.

But I know my future would be brighter,

    if I would just set myself free.

Tribute to the Soul

The BODY awakens to greet each new day,
curious for what lies ahead, work or play.
Once we stretch our sleepy muscles from rest,
we rise to go forth and give it our best.
A marvelous shell for the one living inside,
but a temporal home left empty, when the owner has died.

The MIND directs the body as we stir awake,
guiding us through triumph and every mistake.
Each action is recorded in the well of the brain,
not one deed without it could we abstain.
It is the center of thought, where knowledge increases,
but sadly, a body may live though the mind ceases.

The SOUL is the immortal part of God's plan,
given when God breathed and man began.
A companion made in God's likeness to share eternity,
faith's own image, moral, feeling, and free to be.
There has never been a greater act of giving,
than when God gave man a soul and made him living.

Trust

Bless us, O Lord,

You, Our Maker,

and we the made.

Lest we declare:

"Here is God!"

"Or over there!"

Forgive us, Father,

when as shadow,

we would be shade.

May we dwell,

where placed we are,

and hope for grace,

to cross the bar.

Unemployed

There was a time when I had something to say,
    before my worth and work were gone.

Now, I join the many others who have fallen
    into this empty pit of darkness alone.

I've become a homeless dog that's begging
    from someone else's table,

My suit of pride and self-respect,
    is now a musty cloak of rabble.

What is there left for me now to do,
    what destination becomes my end?

The saddest sight I've ever seen,
    is me peeking around that bend.

Unique, Not Equal

God has no equal,
nor shall man.
Just look at the heaven's
and view their span.
Some stars are bright
and some are dim.
Yet in all their glow,
each belong to Him.
To be one's equal,
is not our task
To fulfill our uniqueness,
is all God asks.

Unwanted!

Get away cur!
you don't belong here.
Things were all calm,
now you appear.
You filthy dog! You smell,
and your legs are all bowed.
Hurry off now,
get on down the road.
Just look at the mess,
your fur is all matted.
Hanging in wads,
where mud is all splattered.
You flea bitten hound,
with pitiful eyes.
Kept me up all night,
with your loud mournful cries.
Go somewhere else,
and beg for bread.
Find another place,
to make your bed.
Good! Run away now,
you mangy sack.
Keep on running,
and never come back.

Upside Down and Inside Out

Sometimes it happens in the night.
I don't believe it is forbidden.
In the dark, it lets in light.
Gathering all in one accord.
Bring to all one earthly sum.
And in the end, Christ is Lord!
Since the beginning was the Word.
Perhaps renewed our hope will come.
Deeds not done bear no reward.
This is precisely why I write.
It was not lost but only hidden.
My early thought has taken flight.

Note:

I wrote this poem: Upside down and inside out.
I did not begin by writing the first line first.
It just came out this way:

Code:

Read line 12 first; line 1 next
then line 11, then line 2
next read 10, then line 3
next read 9, then line 4

and so on.

The last line read should end in Lord!

We Journey Together

Do we only hear
    what we listen for,
        is that how each man grows?

The force that calls each one to act
    was never given as secret truth,
        is that what each man knows?

How arrogant that one
    would speak for God,
        though partial light revealed.

Yet in all the earth
    we hear man's voice,
        where half a bell is pealed.

How little we know or contemplate:
    so few our deeds done well,
        the damaged seeds we've sown.

Without hope; man cries for help,
    if divided he enters that final gate,
        and finds himself alone.

Weathering the Storms

Life is lived in all types of weather,
with many storms passing through.
In due time, the sun always comes out,
and the sky will turn to blue.

When the surge of waters seize you,
or the rain comes pouring down,
just use your faith like a dipper,
and there is no way you will drown.

Remember that in the tempest,
you must be patient until all is clear.
The weather is given for a purpose,
and God is always standing near.

After a storm that you are clearing,
humility will be by your side.
Keep on working until you are finished,
and God will be satisfied.

A team of virtues will attend you,
some you've never known.
In place of all that left you,
you will see how you have grown.

You will build again new places,
another storm is sure to come.
But in each one that you weather,
you will hear the angels strum.

Welcome Little Puppy

A vet was selected,
and all the papers were signed.
The welcome mat is out,
no better home could you find.
There is a cage in the corner,
two dishes by a bed.
Toys are strewn all over,
it's smart to keep them spread.
All the little accidents that sprinkle,
and those land mines along the way,
will soon be forgiven,
as we watch him run and play.
If the others will accept him,
and join me in the fun,
we will all be content,
and our homework will be done.

What Lies Beyond?

I looked past the trees into the dark woods,
    until all grew dark and void of light.
Then I turned my head to face the skies,
    and could not see beyond the night.

What dwells beyond our strength to see,
    or lies beyond that which we know?
Distance does not quell our wanderlust;
    where our souls are beckoned, we long to go.

Would we molest some virgin place;
    should we remain where we are wed?
What cost or risk would we regret,
    if some incurable epidemic spread?

If we should make the journey there,
    and safely arrive with guarantee,
would we return from such a realm,
    where more might be seen from there to we.

What Might Have Been

So many words unspoken,
so many things unsaid.
Questions never asked,
so many hungering for bread.

Walls of chaos, fences for conflict,
dividing up our lives.
Talents untouched, trails never tried,
only overgrown weeds stifling all that strives.

The distance between us,
we may never breach,
if we fail with outstretched arms,
to see how far our hearts can reach.

When I Wake Up

When I wake up with the devil on my shoulder,
I just get down on my knees and pray a little bolder.
God surely will answer for each soul He knows,
is seeded with His mercy as it grows.

There are some things I can handle on my own;
some days it's like nothing can possibly go wrong.
But every now and then that uninvited guest comes around,
and begins to tear up my world and turn it upside down.

Sometimes he appears through a family member or a friend,
tempts me in a weakness, or with a rule he thinks I should bend.
It's not just a little that he bothers me so,
every cell in my body aches, and I just wish that he would go.

He's deceptive, divisive, and downright mean,
spreading rumors and lies and so obscene.
Always seeking out a life to make it his dorm;
just a flittering demon without any form.

I've learned that with patience and prayer I can drive him away,
he hates it when I quote Scripture, then trust and obey.
He never could defeat Jesus, not even in death,
and even in me, dwells God's holy breath.

When Love Is Born

When love is born
    and becomes light,
        it cannot return,
            into the night.

Nor can it cease,
    and dwell alone,
        but seeks the warmth,
            of a welcome home.

When Someone Leaves

When someone leaves you in anger, you ask: "Why?"
And when no answer is given,
the pain makes you die.

How does a person bear being abandoned and alone,
struggling to find the strength to forgive another,
for the harm that was done?

When comfort could have turned a spark into a flame,
you feel the cold chill of winter,
the ice of misguided blame.

Rejected, betrayed, or simply thrown away,
your value is now diminished,
in the mirror you're disfigured with dismay.

Will you rise from the depths of such despair?
Is there help to restore hope within you?
How long until you stand again and really care?

Yet one path you might not have taken:
within your soul you always know,
there is One that hath not forsaken.

Who Is Calling?

I pray a prayer
    when I say out loud
        the thoughts that are in my head.

To someone out there
    I cannot see
        asking for my daily bread.

I express my hopes
    and share my fears,
        or make an honest plea.

Reaching out in solitude
    with thanksgiving and praise,
        to Him who holds eternity.

Will I be heard
    in this highest court
        where every judgment made is clear?

I can rest assured
    because it's not my need,
        but His great Love that called me here.

Whose Crown Shines Brightest?

Clothed in winds sweet whisper,
dew-tipped grass embracing my feet;
nourished by the calm of a restful night,
I stroll about my lavish retreat.

What deed this day may be done by me?
A new morning plan must be unfurled.
Without forethought to gain my way,
I dare not face the world.

Will I a worker or spectator be,
in this garden good and sweet?
Am I here to shepherd the sheep,
or is it my purpose just to eat?

Whose crown will shine brightest,
whose words the last to be hurled,
when all comes to a purposeful end,
who will reign in comfort curled?

Why Poetry?

Poetry misunderstood often seems,

mysterious

delirious

Not making much sense at all?
Verbiage thrown into

broken pots

empty lots

Words planted
where there is not much rain.

Corruptions

Eruptions

Spilling streams of brackish water,
filling wasted shelves.

Mindless chatter

Antique clutter

But once received,
it's growth conceived.

Will You Pray for Me?

So often said; so seldom heard,
when one is genuinely in need of prayer.
Unacceptable is the common or casual word,
for God wants to know you really care.

Preceding every bit of hurt and pain;
even before the diagnosis comes,
prayer ought to flow through every healing vein,
opening up heaven's door with heartfelt strums.

Lest God sees our dirt and grime,
our hands must be washed clean.
Then we may gladly upward climb,
while on our knees to intervene.

The words are few that you must speak;
sweat and blood must course your brow,
before you leave the garden of prayer tired and weak,
assured God bends to hear and make His solemn vow.

Without Stones

A wall not built,

a heart not broken,

a pardon, not guilt,

a life not taken.

Write It Down

Put your words down on paper,
then look and see what you said.
If it ain't what your thinkin',
then you're lyin' to your head.

Write down the things you value,
all the things that can't be bound.
Then let the world come along,
and discover what you found.

Is your record very truthful,
a single lie you would not hide,
every word your signature,
anything less you won't abide?

Is there shame in your contribution,
will it stand the test of time?
Is there a better way of sayin',
what you're writing in your prime?

If you're determined to take your worry,
to the grave with you as you go,
then take the pen and copy,
and sneak away now, no one will know.

Writing Poetry

Writing Poetry

    allows me to dive

        into that bottomless pit

            of self and sorrow,

    until, once again,

  thirsting for life

I begin to rise

    upward toward

        those selfless springs

            of joy.

You Can Be God

Can you speak and watch darkness disappear,
with no regret for what you've begun?
Can you take something formless and empty,
and declare it good when you are done?

Can you create a universe that goes beyond reach,
and make it a speck of sand upon an endless shore?
Can you create everything that exists out of nothing,
and never duplicate it anymore?

Can you create a numberless total,
and place your fullness in the smallest part?
Can you be everywhere both far and near,
possess unlimited power, with knowledge as your art?

Can you make the sun stand still,
and not be confined to time?
Can you always remain the same,
while all else becomes a changing rhyme?

Can you give out of emptiness,
and pour water from a stone?
Can you offer an endless supply,
a gift sufficient for everyone?

Can you own absolutely everything,
yet give it all away?
Can you answer every question,
never regretting what you have to say?

Can you make laws that stand forever,
laws that no one can dispute?
Can you resist all temptation,
and through any trial remain resolute?

Can you erase every act of wrong,
and replace it with one act of right?
Can you speak a word of forgiveness,
and give the blind back his sight?

Can you pass through death and live again,
restoring life for those who die,
Can you make out of the End a new Beginning,
while all about you cry: "Glorify!"

Can you make man from a piece of sod?
If you can, then you can be God!

"The fool hath said in his heart, there is no God" (Ps. 14:1).

About the Author

Ken Turbyfill was born in the mountains of North Carolina, just after the Great Depression. The second of six sons of an itinerant Baptist preacher, himself, feeling the call at the age of eight, baptized at sixteen, and determined to become the next Billy Graham. Thinking that he might also like to become a career Marine, he signed up immediately after high school. Following a life-changing experience of the Vietnam War, he soon married, became the father of two children, and finding it difficult to keep the same job more than a few weeks or months, decided on the need to invest his anxieties in furthering his education. With studies completed, he entered into full-time ministry as a pastor where he served four churches, worked as an evangelist, and missionary at every opportunity. He now resides in North Carolina where he travels throughout the state living in both the mountains and the beach. Poetry has been a passion of his for many years.